HUGH GAITSKELL

1906–1963

HUGH GAITSKELL

1906–1963

Edited by

W. T. RODGERS MP

LONDON
THAMES AND HUDSON

Printed in Great Britain by The Camelot Press Limited,
London and Southampton

CONTENTS

INTRODUCTION

At 9.12 on the evening of Friday, 18 January, 1963, at the Middlesex Hospital in London, Hugh Gaitskell died. It had been a day of increasing strain. On the Wednesday night an artificial kidney had been used to relieve new and serious complications in his illness. There had been some response, but the Friday morning bulletin said that a heart weakness was giving rise to great anxiety and that his condition remained critical. He was conscious all day and appeared to be resting. The end came quickly. A brief statement issued afterwards by the hospital secretary said: 'Mr. Gaitskell's heart condition deteriorated suddenly and he died peacefully.' His death was later found to have been due to an unusual fulminating form of lupus erythematosis, a rare disease of the tissues, difficult to diagnose and impossible permanently to cure.

1962 had been an exceedingly busy year for Hugh Gaitskell with frequent trips abroad, strenuous negotiations on the Common Market and the sharpening of political controversy at home. On 4 December he returned from Paris where he had been seeing the French Prime Minister and Foreign Minister and the next day complained of a rheumatic pain in his left shoulder. For ten days, however, he continued with his normal routine of a dozen or more engagements a day, as well as Parliamentary business. On Thursday, 13 December, he was in his usual place in the House of Commons at 3.15

for Prime Minister's questions and later that evening intervened briefly in a debate on the latest negotiations with the
Six at Brussels. But the following morning he telephoned
his doctor, Sir John Nicolson, and arranged to call later in
the day at Manor House Hospital. In the event, he returned
straight home from the House of Commons, went to bed,
and was seen there by Sir John at 6 p.m. He complained
of feeling generally unwell and of pains in his joints, and
showed symptoms of a chest infection. Arrangements were
accordingly made to admit him to Manor House Hospital the
next day, 15 December. Thus began the struggle for life which
was to last just over a month.

At Manor House, Hugh Gaitskell was seen by three doctors
who found him to be suffering from virus pneumonia. He
remained in bed, although working and seeing many visitors;
and within a week the condition had cleared. He was pro-
nounced fit to accept an invitation from Mr. Kruschev to
visit Moscow and on 23 December was discharged from
hospital and allowed to go home. But that evening there was
a relapse: his temperature rose to 100 and he suffered from
more generalized pains than hitherto. On Boxing Day,
the Soviet Ambassador was summoned to his home at 18
Frognal Gardens and saw Mr. Gaitskell in the presence of Sir
John Nicolson. He was told that the trip was now off.

During the next few days Mr. Gaitskell was seen by the
Queen's physician, Dr. Bodley Scott, who confirmed that he
was still suffering from a prolonged virus infection associated
with pneumonia. But in view of his general condition it was
decided to move him to Middlesex Hospital where the facilities
for further investigation were second to none. He was taken
there by ambulance through deep snow on 4 January and
until his death occupied a private room on the first floor of
the Woolavington wing overlooking the gardens of the hospital.

Henceforth, Hugh Gaitskell's illness was closely followed both at home and abroad. Anxiety increased as his condition remained persistently serious. In the last week, newspapermen were permanently stationed at the hospital and every radio and television bulletin carried news of the latest developments. Hundreds of telegrams were received and cables came from all over the world. Gifts of flowers were regularly arriving and telephone wires to the hospital were blocked by incoming enquiries to the special information office that had been set up. When the time came, his death was announced to the waiting reporters by Mr. John Harris, the Labour Party's Press Officer. Mr. Gaitskell, he said, 'had put up a tremendous fight for life. The doctors said that they had rarely seen such courage.' Within minutes of his death, the BBC and ITV had interrupted their programmes to make the announcement, and the news had already been flashed round the world. Mr. Harold Wilson, who was to succeed Mr. Gaitskell as Leader of the Labour Party, returned to his New York hotel from a visit to United Nations headquarters to find press representatives already assembled barely twenty minutes after the announcement at the Middlesex Hospital. By the morning, flags were flying at half-mast on churches and public buildings throughout Britain.

The deep public concern with which his illness was followed and the sense of tragedy on his death were remarkable in the apparent circumstances. Hugh Gaitskell had been Leader of the Opposition for only seven years. He was still a man of middle years with no pre-emptive claim to the respect which old age earns, even in politics. He had served, more than a decade before, for barely a year in the Cabinet, leaving no monument of legislation by which to be remembered. He had been a controversial figure, not only and inevitably in the country as the leader of a great Party, but also within his own Party. He had not been thrust into the public eye by the sort of abnormal war conditions which enhance reputations. Nor had his rise to leadership in the Labour Movement been a romance of poverty and hardship overcome.

Hugh Gaitskell was born at Campden Hill, Kensington, on 9 April, 1906. His father had joined the Indian Civil Service straight from Oxford, and was to serve all his time in Burma. The Gaitskells came from Cumberland, but moved south and settled in Bermondsey—then on the rural outskirts of London —in the eighteenth century. Family history has it that Colonel Thomas Gaitskell, a Deputy-Lieutenant and magistrate, raised a militia in Napoleonic times and it is certain that there was a strong family tradition of military service. On his mother's side, Hugh Gaitskell's line can be traced back to Dr. William Garrow, who was surgeon to Queen Anne and whose nephew served in Parliament. The family came from Banffshire in Scotland and were mostly farmers, although Hugh's maternal grandfather did so well at the village school that he went on to Aberdeen University.

As a child, Hugh Gaitskell spent some time in Burma, but when he was nine his father died, aged forty-five, from a tropical disease. Four years later his mother married again and returned to Burma. Thereafter, his school holidays were spent with his brother and sister or with relatives. His elder brother Arthur, to whom he was very attached throughout his life, and who preceded him to Winchester and New College, went to a job in the Sudan in 1922, and it was confidently expected that Hugh would follow into public service abroad. When he eventually announced that this was not his intention his mother wept. This was an unlikely background even for the economics lecturer he first became: it was particularly improbable for the future leader of the Labour Movement.

How was it, then, that Hugh Gaitskell emerged from this conventional middle-class environment to become a political figure greatly respected not only in Britain but throughout the world? What gave his early death the proportions of a major tragedy and left such a hollow gap in the lives of those who were close to him?

This book is intended to go some way towards answering these questions. Although a tribute to his memory, it goes beyond warm affection and respectful praise. It is certainly not a work of hagiography carefully designed to exclude any breath of doubt or criticism. It would diminish rather than enhance Hugh Gaitskell to treat him so. On the other hand, it is not a comprehensive narrative of his life, with all the details written in. There are gaps and omissions and sometimes the same event is touched upon by several authors. The book is essentially an interim biography, showing the course and manner of his intellectual and political development from early manhood into the years of power and responsibility. As Sir Maurice Bowra says, Hugh Gaitskell developed to maturity 'in a singularly straight line'. But one theme which recurs constantly is the way he revealed at every turn a new dimension hitherto unsuspected. It is part of the tragedy of his death that it cut short a process of unfolding that would have taken him far beyond his already great achievements. The full story of his life and a final assessment of him as a man and as a public figure must await another book. There is much more that could be said, for example, of the influence on him of his wife and family in whom he found great love and enjoyment. Meanwhile, this will serve both as a portrait of him by his friends and, in a wider sense, as a footnote to the history of our time.

Most of the contributors to this book are either of Hugh Gaitskell's own generation or from amongst those who shared closely with him the experience of an important part of his life. Perhaps it is appropriate that the editor should be of the generation which came of age after he had already served in government and knew him mainly at a distance. For in the sharpest controversy of Hugh Gaitskell's life, the fierce dispute in the Labour Party over defence in 1960 and 1961, many young people found themselves ranged against him. It may have been inevitable that the proper rebelliousness of thoughtful young people should have set many of them in opposition to the leadership of the Party on a terrifying, complex and frustrating issue. The youngest voter today was born in the year of the Beveridge Report and was three when the 1945 Labour Government came in. He is quite without memories of the pre-war world. It is not the achievements of the government in which Hugh Gaitskell served that he remembers or the precarious balance of peace which followed the proud hopes of Potsdam and San Francisco. He is bothered instead by a divided world apparently unable to stop the race to catastrophe. On the question of nuclear disarmament a collision between generations was hard to avoid.

But this is not the whole story and it would be wrong to allow a legend to grow up that Hugh Gaitskell was unsympathetic in the eyes of younger people of his own party. It can be argued, and indeed it is in places in this book, that he was not always skilled in the finer arts of political management. There may have been conflicts that could have been avoided by greater flexibility and less stubbornness. But it is precisely the extent to which he was an 'unprofessional' politician that made him so attractive and reassuring. Here was a man of real intellectual distinction and great strength of character who had reached the top through none of the devious stratagems which so often seem to be a necessary passport to success. Through Hugh Gaitskell our faith was strengthened not only in the non-doctrinal socialist tradition of conscience and reform but in the system itself. He took the cynicism out of the conduct of politics. That, at least, was my own experience and it was how many of my friends and associates felt.

Perhaps the best description of the approach to politics that so attracted us is to be found in Hugh Gaitskell's own words. In an introduction to Evan Durbin's *Politics of Democratic Socialism* he described the views of the group of Durbin's friends in the 1930s of whom he himself had been one:

> The most fundamental ideal of those who shared this outlook was social justice—but it was an ideal in no way inspired by class hatred. They were equally devoted to democracy and personal freedom. They believed in tolerance and they understood the need for compromise. They were for the rational and the practical, and suspicious of large general ideas which on examination turned out to have no precise content. They were scornful of those who were content to talk. They wanted to get results . . . They were realistic in politics and critical of armchair politicians who, not understanding what the British electorate was really like, were for ever making bad political judgements. Above all, while accepting the ultimate emotional basis of moral valuation, they had great faith in the power of reason both to find the answers to social problems and to persuade men to see the light. They were for the pursuit of truth to the bitter end, through the patient and unswerving application of logical thought. They wanted no barriers of prejudice to obstruct the free working of the mind or blunt the sharp edge of intellectual integrity.

Here we see Hugh Gaitskell himself and the spirit that has left many of us in his debt.

I am particularly grateful to Hugh Gaitskell's widow, Mrs. Dora Gaitskell, and also to his sister Lady Ashton and his brother Mr. Arthur Gaitskell for kindness and patience when I have sought their help and advice. Mr. Ivan Yates generously read the whole book in proof. Responsibility for the contents and for the final shape of the book remains mine alone.

November 1963   W. T. RODGERS

SCHOOL DAYS AND AFTER

John Betjeman

I first knew Hugh Gaitskell when we were boys together at
Lynam's (The Dragon School, Oxford), a school mostly for
the sons of professional people and Oxford dons. There was
something remarkable about this school, which made it stand
out from the more conventional establishments among the
private schools of England. The Headmaster, 'The Skipper'
(C. C. Lynam), who was there during an early formative part
of Hugh's life as a schoolboy was an unconventional man who
dressed like a merchant seaman, wore a red tie and was an
early socialist. His views caused him to admit to the school not
just service people and the sons of dons who had inherited
the 'first class brains' of their parents, but also the sons of
Oxford tradesmen. There were also a few girls to teach us
courtesy to the opposite sex. The atmosphere of the school was
free and easy. Dress was unconventional for the times. There
was no marching in 'crocodiles'. Games were not compulsory.
We could go into the town on our bicycles. There were
expeditions in an old Ford van the Skipper owned, and on
bicycles, to the countryside which then existed round Oxford.
All the world seemed at our feet. I remember a friend telling
me that Hugh Gaitskell told him, many years later, that once
when they were going past North Parade, the street of little

shops to which we went to buy the sweets after lunch, Hugh remarked, 'This is where I first became a socialist.' He pointed out that it was there, looking at these little shops in a parade of small houses, which contrasted with the big Gothic Revival detached houses in North Oxford around it, he was made aware that some people were not so well off as others. It was in the nature of an Evangelical conversion. There were politically minded boys at the school at the time, including Lance and Percival Mallalieu, sons of the Liberal MP for the Colne Valley (and now themselves Labour Members of the House of Commons).

Hugh, I remember in the school holidays, as a tidily dressed boy who lived in one of those big houses in South Kensington —in Onslow Gardens, I think—when they were still private houses and had not been turned into flats. His family had a long record of service to the country in India. I have found tablets to his Gaitskell forbears of the ICS in the tower of Christ Church, Cheltenham (the spa which was the retiring place of so many Service people,) and in the old parish church of Lewisham. I dare say his reaction against this traditional and conventional upper-middle-class background was encouraged by the liberal spirit of his preparatory school. But to his background at home he owed the strong sense of public duty which lasted all his life. Hugh Gaitskell was really a public servant, as his forbears had been before him, but a servant of socialist principles.

I met him when we were both undergraduates at Oxford, with our friend Lionel Perry, at the dinner parties of Maurice Bowra, who was then Dean of Wadham. Hugh still looked exactly the same as he had done at Lynam's, with curly hair and the habit of suddenly blushing. I must confess that I never thought of him then as a politically minded person. To me and to most friends, Oxford then was not divided into 'Left and Right', but into 'Aesthetes' and 'Hearties'. 'Hearties' played games, drank beer and were full of college and team spirit and wore club ties and tweeds. 'Aesthetes' never played games, drank wine and liqueurs, never went into their colleges more than they could help and wore plain silk ties and elegant cloth suits. Hugh was certainly more an 'Aesthete' than a 'Hearty', though he never dressed as one. He retained the influence of Winchester in his way of making words noticeably disyllabic: 'cha-pel'; 'li-ttle'.

Hugh was a gentle and kind person who had no objection to a drop of drink and was very easy company and full of jokes. He was interested in people. He was the reverse of a 'hearty' and therefore a friend of mine. It was for these reasons and not because we had both been at Lynam's that we were friends. Now I come to think of it, there were always times when the old thing talked on for hours, after those wonderful uproarious dinner parties of Maurice Bowra's, about statistics and economics and politics, but I did not listen much. He was as much interested in art and literature, and joined in these discussions too. It is a measure of his tolerance that he never obtruded his political views on non-political friends, nor thought less of them because they were uninterested in politics.

The Oxford of our day was just before the big slump, and many undergraduates still had large allowances from their fathers. Having a good time was more important than getting a degree. At this period Hugh, because of his political opinions, lived on 10*d.* a day and ate at fried fish shops and got a good degree.

I became aware of him as someone more than the usual Oxford aesthete at the time of the General Strike. 'Aesthetes', as the intellectuals and rebels, were temperamentally on the side of the strikers. 'Hearties' manned the public services. Under G. D. H. Cole and his wife, Margaret, from their house in Holywell, Hugh organized his friends to help the strikers. I remember that Lionel Perry, John Dugdale and I were sent, in John Dugdale's Morris, to Didcot to take messages for the strikers there. I do not recall their having any messages for us to take. The gesture, however, was made. To Hugh and John the General Strike was not the lark it was to me. It was in a righteous cause. Just before I was sent down from Oxford, I took over Hugh's old rooms in Isis Street, an unfashionable, but attractive working-class street, with houses looking over the river at Folly Bridge.

In 1929, when Hugh was living in a flat in Great Ormond Street, near his work at University College, London, Lionel Perry and I were houseless and I was penniless and without a job. It was characteristic of Hugh that he allowed us to share the flat with him rent free for several weeks. It was in these days that he met his future wife, Dora.

These facts do not really give the picture of him I would wish to convey, which is that of a loyal, pleasure-loving, warm, humorous and generous friend. The friends of his Oxford days remained so to the end of his life. His loved and loving Dora accepted them as part of him and they used to have excellent parties in their house in Frognal Gardens, with wine and laughter and Maurice Bowra at the top of his form. Hugh genuinely enjoyed the fame that came to him towards the end of his life. Most of all he enjoyed the company of those who loved him. He inspired affection because he was an emotional person who gave out sympathy and practical help. I cannot remember particular conversations or any brilliant remarks, not because he never made the latter nor because the former were uninteresting. I was so used to him and took him for granted as part of my life that I did not bother to recall what he said. I basked, as did all his friends, in his gentle good-heartedness and was always assured of his loyalty and understanding.

OXFORD IN THE NINETEEN TWENTIES

Maurice Bowra

Hugh Gaitskell was in his first year as an undergraduate at New
College, Oxford, when I came to know him. It was the winter
of 1924–5. We had friends in common from whom I had
heard of him as someone whom they all liked, but when I met
him I was surprised that I had not heard more. He was eighteen
years old, slim, curly-haired and fresh-coloured, and had not
yet developed any of the prominent features which were to
delight caricaturists in his later years. He was lively, cheerful,
even ebullient, entirely at his ease without being in the least
aggressive or conceited. He was clearly intelligent, but he was
not a scholar trained to a single, dominating discipline, nor did
he move in the company of Wykehamist scholars who had
come to Oxford at the same time as himself. He had not much
enjoyed Winchester, and it never meant much to him. Oxford
brought him a deliverance from much that had hitherto
cramped and inhibited him, and he gave himself to it with all
the thrill of a new discovery.

He made his own circle of friends with a discriminating
insight, but they were not at all of one kind. It was characteristic of him then, as later, that he did not think it necessary to
bring them together. Perhaps his closest friend was Evan
Durbin, whom to my great regret I never met, but he was also

on affectionate terms with people as varied as W. H. Auden, John Betjeman, John Sparrow, Jim Orrick, Duff Dunbar and Frank Pakenham. He had a lively taste for social life, not of the rowdier undergraduate kind, but at least for food and drink and uninhibited conversation. At a time when women at Oxford were kept almost in purdah, and association with them earned the disapproval of the young and the darkest suspicions of the old, he had the acquaintance of some highly attractive and intelligent girls, although even then he tended to reserve their company for privileged occasions, such as Eights Week and Commemoration Balls. He moved with an easy and entirely instinctive tact from one circle to another and was at home and welcome in all. There were indeed limits to his sociability. He mixed only with those whom he liked and was as far as possible from losing himself in too many acquaintances. But those whom he liked, he liked a great deal, and they liked him in return.

At this stage of his career Hugh might have been thought to be no more remarkable than a number of other young men who have charm and intelligence and a strong interest in their fellow-beings. What made him different even then was that he was all of a piece, that he was not only entirely natural and straightforward but that he lacked those inner conflicts which disturb so many young people. He had indeed his conflicts, but they were issues which called for decisions, and these by thought and insight he was able to make. At his centre was his unusual warmth of heart, his real care for other people, his desire to keep them happy, and this made him happy with them. He took very seriously the troubles of his friends and was often able to solve them by simple common sense. He liked talk not only because it engaged his faculties but because it cleared the air of convention and cant, and if a party was more than usually convivial, there was always a chance that the talk would be freer and more honest than at other times.

The respect and affection which his friends felt for him was largely due to their conviction that he was entirely loyal, that he would do anything for them, that he had even in his inexperienced youth an instinctive understanding of them. His understanding had of course its limits. He was drawn to people with lively minds and an active taste for living, and he was never at home with the solemn or the pompous. Nor in the last resort was he much interested in the subtler refinements of psychology. For him there was quite enough to be done with the ordinary problems of human beings without troubling about such enquiries, and even though he was from an early date interested in psycho-analysis, it was because he saw in it a valuable means for alleviating certain kinds of suffering. He nursed an ideal of happiness for himself and for others, and that others might have it he was willing to exert himself to the utmost. Such an ideal was reached not through any philosophical studies, though it was to gain strength from them, but from his own nature which convinced him without further argument that it was foolish to look for anything else.

In all this there was of course a sense of purpose, partly unconscious and certainly not yet explicit, but at least latent and likely to find some suitable goal. When Oxford engaged Hugh Gaitskell's intelligence, as his school had failed to do, it set him on a path from which he never turned back and provided him with the intellectual framework which he needed to set his other gifts harmoniously to work.

He was one of the very first men to read the new Honours School of Philosophy, Politics, and Economics. This course, devised by A. D. Lindsay and others who felt that academic studies could profitably be brought closer to the actual working of society without losing their disciplinary virtues, had not been brought into existence without considerable alarms and misgivings. There was, it was claimed, a shortage of teachers; the three subjects would not consort happily together;

standards would be uncertain, and, anyhow, was the modern world a proper subject for study? Fortunately 'Modern Greats', as some unknown supporter ably named it, engaged the loyalty of a few gifted teachers and attracted undergraduates who were less interested in the past than in the present and felt that the mere study of history did not give them that background of theory which their intelligence needed. In its early days the new course had an almost missionary fervour, as its supporters strove to show that it was at once difficult and exhilarating. It was much to Hugh Gaitskell's credit that he decided at the start to read it, and he took to it with avidity. If philosophy never meant very much to him, economics and politics, in the sense of government, meant a great deal. He was never boring about his studies and did not talk 'shop' unless he was certain that it would be welcome, but 'Modern Greats' was a solid, even a central part of Hugh's life, and he managed to work hard at it without sacrificing other interests.

A contemporary of his at New College, who made the same choice, was Frank Pakenham, who was then a pillar of the Carlton Club and a devoted admirer of Lord Birkenhead. He and Hugh were entirely happy in each other's company, and sharpened each other's wits from their increasingly opposed points of view. They learned much from their tutor, H. K. Salvesen, who disagreed with both and provoked them to challenge his opinions.

The study of economics and politics provided Hugh Gaitskell with the solid foundation which he needed to justify his natural, instinctive convictions. As soon as he began to think about the world around him, he found that it outraged both his feelings and his intelligence. The 1914–18 war was temporarily forgotten, and the mood of exhaustion which followed it was beginning to yield to uneasy questionings. Mr. Baldwin had begun his long tenure of power and offered a sleepy, insular peace built on social inequalities, prolonged unemployment, and a distrust of any political thinking. This repelled Hugh Gaitskell, as it repelled those of his elders who now began to feel that the war had been fought to no purpose, and it forced him to look at politics from first principles and increasing convictions. His natural tenderness was outraged by the sordid and brutal conditions in which a large part of the population lived; his sense of order and decency was appalled by the jungle of a competitive system in which the few had too much and the many too little; his sharp and honest mind was not deceived by the opiates handed out by the Prime Minister to persuade men that all was well.

In these conditions Hugh formed the beliefs which were to govern his later political life. He read Marx, but was not much impressed by him. He thought Marxism too mechanical to be right and too inhuman to deserve any devotion. Nor did he think that history had justified some of Marx's more famous prophecies or that the Russia of the Soviets had any qualities of an earthly paradise. Nor was he, like Lansbury and Attlee, a Christian Socialist, who based his plans for reform on a practical interpretation of Gospel precepts. He had abandoned Christianity at school and never reverted to it. Its religious side meant nothing to him and he found its ethics too vague and too subjective to inspire any practical course of action. His politics were based, quite simply, on two main elements in himself: his natural charity and his critical intelligence. If he was deeply distressed by suffering or injustice, he was shocked by what seemed to him the appalling waste and incompetence of existing society. He wanted human beings to be themselves, and he felt that they were prevented by ghoulish dogmas which had no rational roots.

In forming his political views, Hugh Gaitskell was much helped and guided by G. D. H. Cole, and was himself always the first to say so. Cole, who had had a brilliant career at Oxford before the war, came back in 1924 as Reader in

Economics. His appointment was denounced by the Vice-Chancellor in his inaugural speech—fortunately in the decent obscurity of academic Latin—and it certainly caused pain to some elderly dons who thought that Cole had behaved badly in the war, of which he did not approve, and was likely to corrupt the young. Cole was a delightful and unusually gifted man. Despite long ill health, he was an indefatigable worker, not merely a learned expert in his own wide field but extremely well read in a wide range of history and literature. Though he changed his views on what socialism ought to be, he remained a dedicated socialist and became the inspiring guide of a small circle of clever young men who shared his main convictions, but needed his help in thinking out what they meant in practice. He was transparently honest, courageous and generous. He was as incapable of hiding disapproval as of refusing to admit his own mistakes. Hugh Gaitskell saw in him somebody after his own heart and Cole formed a lasting affection for Gaitskell. Cole strengthened Hugh's natural generosity and tolerance by his own firmly founded views and opened to him a wide scope of reading, by no means all on political matters, of which Gaitskell had been unaware. Cole's equable temper in times of crisis, his lack of resentment or vanity, his striking sincerity set an example to his friends which they felt impelled to follow. Cole, partly from reasons of health, did not share all Gaitskell's livelier tastes, but he certainly did not disapprove, regarding them as right in a healthy and vigorous young man. Cole enjoyed work and taught others to enjoy it with him, and to him Gaitskell owed much of that taste for work which carried him through his career. Cole preached a thorough-going socialism, and this was what Gaitskell was looking for. It answered the calls alike of his heart and his head, and in Cole's quiet but passionate approach to living problems Gaitskell found an example for himself. He was, of course, much more a man of action than Cole, but his actions now conformed to a pattern which he had largely learned from his master.

The proof of Hugh Gaitskell's new command of himself and of the direction in which he was moving came in May 1926 with the General Strike. The news of it burst suddenly on an astonished Oxford, just settling down to enjoy the Summer Term. The national call for help meant that many dons and almost all undergraduates rushed off to strike-breaking activities. Since the TUC was thought to have defied not only Mr. Baldwin but the whole system of constitutional government, the case for the strikers had little chance of a benevolent hearing, especially as some of their own leaders had grave doubts about the wisdom of their action. When most undergraduates were rushing off to what they thought might be sensational adventures, Hugh stayed in Oxford and worked for the strikers. He admitted that the TUC might have made an error of judgement, but he insisted that this was no cause for the violent campaign now being waged against the trade unions or for any brutalities which might all too easily be committed. He was not going to desert his side just because it had miscalculated its means, and he was certainly not going to join the vociferous rowdies who clamoured for reprisals. He was not in the least self-assertive about his action, but set about it with a quiet determination, not caring what others might think of him. In fact his behaviour was so unusual and so unexpected that it disarmed criticism. College authorities, like his own Warden, H. A. L. Fisher, who profoundly disapproved of the strike, found themselves respecting his sincerity and wondering if they might not perhaps have done the same thing in their less regenerate days. The crisis soon passed, and everyone came back to work, but Hugh Gaitskell had avoided the great refusal and made the great decision. He had committed himself to a cause, and he was never to abandon it afterwards.

The General Strike greatly strengthened Hugh Gaitskell's confidence in himself. Politics became his chief interest; he knew something about it and talked freely about it. He was not in the least afraid of discussing political matters with people who held views very different from his own; though in such discussions he often got delightfully excited, he never lost his temper or his manners or his control of the subject. Indeed, the very force of his feelings concentrated his powers and helped him to state his case with a greater cogency and concentration. Once at dinner with me he met a young and rich coal-owner, a man of much charm and tolerance but inexorably attached to the owners' point of view. In a very short time he and Hugh Gaitskell were at it for all that they were worth, and continued to argue most of the evening. Then for the first time I realised how formidable Hugh's capacity had become in conducting an argument on a highly technical matter which called for knowledge, subtlety and skill. Fortunately, my friend liked him from the start and the debate was amicable and even gay, but Hugh refused to yield any point or to make any compromise. He stood up, making those gestures which were to be so familiar in later years, when he knocked down a flimsy argument or rammed a point home. His opponent certainly was no rival in intellectual power, but he knew his subject from the inside and put up a good case for it. What was really impressive was the spectacle of Hugh Gaitskell's mind fully at work, in complete control of the material, and yet so quick on the uptake that he could deal at once with any new and unforeseen point. Just as in later years his speeches were remarkable for their clarity and force and indeed for the sheer hard thinking behind them, so even at this date the same qualities were impressively present.

It was no surprise that in the summer of 1927 Hugh took a first class in his Final Schools. He had not only worked hard and thought for himself, but he had organized his time-table with some skill and by no means sacrificed his other enjoyments to the call of work. He could switch without noticing it from work to relaxation, and to each he gave all his energies with a whole-hearted attention.

In August 1927 Hugh Gaitskell and I went for a holiday on the Adriatic. He certainly needed it after the efforts and ardours of Final Schools, and, though he had been abroad before, this part of the world was new to him, and he responded to it with delight. He was an excellent travelling companion, ready to enjoy all manner of sights and people and quite uncomplaining about such discomforts as then disturbed the peace of such places as Pola and Parenzo. Travelling on deck to Split we both thought that we were dying of cholera, and were much surprised and delighted when on landing we met W. H. Auden, whose father, a doctor, cured us with strong doses of Dr. Collis Brown. Hugh enjoyed above all the sun and the sea, but did not take them too lazily. He practised diving for whole mornings on end, insisted that a long siesta was not necessary, made friends with an Austrian who had a boat and with whom we explored coves and islands along the coast south of Dubrovnik.

On man-made objects Hugh was more selective. We began our tour in Venice, but it did not greatly appeal to him. He thought it too grand and too showy and I also suspect that his social conscience made him dislike the Venetians of the great age. In Yugoslavia he was much more at home. Indeed, to the end of his life he thought Dubrovnik the most delightful place he had ever seen and returned to it more than once. He certainly liked its unobtrusive elegance, but he also felt that the Yugoslavs even in those days were real as the Venetians were not. His aesthetic sense was busily at work, and he kept his eyes open for such new sights as the mausoleum built by Mestrovic at Cavtat. It was perhaps characteristic of him that he was not interested in the spacious remains of the Palace of Diocletian as smacking too much of authority or because he actually disliked it. In later years he learned to enjoy the arts more for their own sake, but at this time his taste for them was strongly shaped by his sense of history and his social conscience. If Dubrovnik won his love, it was quite as much for its tough, independent inhabitants as for the beauty of its white walls over the sea.

On our return we stopped at Vienna, which Hugh had visited before and greatly liked, partly because it was governed by an efficient socialist council, partly because it provided the kind of night-life which he most enjoyed, that is night-clubs which were not showy or expensive and encouraged dancing to be taken seriously. He was not troubled by the *Schlamperei* of Vienna, which was markedly in evidence in most public services, but he was already interested in the social and economic troubles of Austria and as yet not hostile to the *Anschluss* with Germany, which was a common topic of conversation. He had indeed, like others of his generation, a certain softness for the Germans and was himself a little prone to the dangerous guilt which many English had begun to feel about the Treaty of Versailles. He saw both the Germans and the Austrians as honest democrats struggling to keep their countries alive and free, but hampered by the statesmen of France and Great Britain. In this there was a certain measure of truth, but Hugh was certainly blind to the dark forces at work in both peoples and did not welcome gloomy forecasts that democracy could not last in either country. Later he was to admit that he had been wrong. He was deeply distressed when Dollfuss and Starhemberg slaughtered the socialists in Vienna, and he did his best to help the distressed by making their sufferings known to the world.

He had something of the same experience with the Germans. He admired their efficiency, their industry and their taste for the arts, and for a time he much preferred them to the French and the Italians. Then when Hitler came to power, he saw at once the appalling monstrosity of the whole Nazi nightmare and made no excuses for it. But in such matters he tended to try to be just and at the start to see both sides of a question fairly and squarely before making up his mind. This quality, which he never lost, led him sometimes to be called pusillanimous, but in fact it was simply a determination not to come to a decision until he had found out all that he could and then passed judgement on it. Once his mind was made up, he stuck to it and was ready with all the answers. This was to make him a formidable critic of opponents who had made up their minds more rapidly, but had not thought out their cases so carefully.

I saw quite a lot of Hugh Gaitskell after he left Oxford. He would come to stay with me there, and I stayed with him first in Nottingham and later in London. He matured rapidly, learned from experience, and extended his knowledge of men and things. Yet he remained very much the same charming, natural, honest, gay person. It was his intention to pursue an academic career, which should have a strong political bias, and in this he was much influenced by Cole's example. He did not yet realise how formidable his gifts for action were, how easily his speeches could hold an audience, how men and women not of his own background could like and trust him. On the other hand he began to have doubts whether he ought really to be a don. He was in fact a very good one—not merely hard-working and serious, but much interested in his pupils and more than willing to help them and make the best of them. His promotion to London was certainly a tribute to his teaching abilities and he might well have made a career there. The war put an end to it, and after the war, during which I hardly saw him, he committed himself finally to politics. I met him again on 31 December, 1945, and we picked up our relations just where the war had broken them off. After that I saw a lot of him and watched his rise to power and fame with gratitude and admiration. He was entirely unspoiled by office or success; he was still his old self, wiser and more tolerant but no less happy and at peace with himself. There were times when he wondered whether he should not have stuck to the academic life, but he would conclude that he would not perhaps be very good at it. Such modesty was part of his nature. He was never hard on dons, because he had himself been one. Indeed he kept to the last a passionate interest in university matters and his views on them were closely reasoned and far-reaching.

Hugh Gaitskell developed naturally from boyhood to maturity in a singularly straight line. The qualities which made him so effective in politics were already present in his undergraduate days—the intelligence, the determination, the candour, the courage. So too were those other qualities which won not only the love of his friends but the admiration of many who did not know him but saw that he was a profoundly good man. Beyond all these were others no less remarkable—his love of life, his need and capacity for affection, his taste for all things which keep men awake and alive to the endless possibilities of the world about them. He had wings and a harp . . . .

DISCOVERING THE LABOUR MOVEMENT

Margaret Cole

I have been asked to write about the part of Hugh Gaitskell's life during which I knew him, politically and personally, perhaps as well as anyone now living except his closest friends, and during which he grew from an exceptionally intelligent undergraduate with some leanings towards social change to a man who, if he took seriously to politics, was fairly sure to become, if not party leader or Prime Minister, at least an important member of a Labour administration if and when it should come into being. Those years, therefore, from 1925, when my husband returned to Oxford with his family as Reader in Economics and tutor of University College, to about the end of 1934, when Gaitskell came back to England after his unexpectedly exciting term as Rockefeller Research Fellow in Vienna and began to try seriously to influence the international policies of the Labour Party, may well have been one of the key periods of his whole career.

I cannot claim that when I first met Gaitskell I 'spotted' him as a future leader of the Labour Party; in fact, I have no recollection at all of our initial meeting. As he was not at University College, it is not likely that he came to any of the weekly lunches which we gave to undergraduates, since these were primarily attended by Douglas's own pupils; nor can I remember that he attended any of the evening discussions of socialist undergraduates which we started at our home in Holywell almost as soon as we had arrived in Oxford—these were the discussions which long afterwards came to be known as the Cole Group, and went on for over thirty years, long after we had ceased to live in Oxford. They are generally agreed to have played a large part in forming the 'climate of Labour opinion', at any rate until the formation of the 1945 Labour Government; but Gaitskell played little part in them at the beginning. My first clear recollection of him is at the wheel of a little snub-nosed Morris car belonging to the father of John Dugdale—another of Douglas's pupils—on a May morning of 1926, driving along the Henley road to London and passing on the way long trains stationary on the Great Western line. For this was the second or third day of the General Strike, and Gaitskell was taking me, as liaison representative of the Oxford University Strike Committee, to pick up supplies of the *British Worker*—the Labour strike paper—and circulars and instructions from the TUC headquarters in Eccleston Square.

Hugh himself always pointed to the General Strike, and the contacts he made as a result of it, as the chief turning-point in his life. This is very true, and not merely for the obvious reason that through it he first discovered 'the organised Labour movement'. To understand its full significance one has to recreate mentally the whole political atmosphere of England, Oxford and Labour in those far-off days. For England as a whole—and for Oxford—by the autumn of 1924, when Hugh came up to New College from Winchester, the most important fact was that the world war was over, and not only the war, but its immediate aftermath—the paper boom and the 'industrial unrest', temporarily arousing Left-wing hopes, to which it had given rise. 'Never again' was still the almost universal conviction.

It is not always clearly remembered today that in 1919 it was war itself that was never to come again, whereas in 1945 it was the horrors of peace, unemployment, the dole and the Poor Law, which were to be prevented at all costs—hence, largely, the Labour landslide among those who had been told to *Ask Your Dad*. And by 1925 it looked, to those who observed and who wrote the newspapers, as though that conviction was on the way to being justified. The worst results of the Versailles Treaty seemed to be mitigated with the ending of the French occupation of the Ruhr and the acceptance of the Dawes Plan on reparations; the tiresome little new nations were settling down, and the League of Nations and the ILO getting into their stride; only a small minority was really excited about Mussolini, and Hitler had retreated into oblivion.

So, also, in Oxford. The difficult ex-Army undergraduates, with their wounds, their war-gratuities which melted so fast, and their painful consciousness of premature ageing and un-shared and uncommunicable experience, had passed through and were gone. The general loosening-up of manners, the product of wartime and the semi-emancipation of women, however slight that may seem in comparison with the 'sixties, had brought about a change which was not reversed when war conditions came to an end. A new generation had arrived, rejoicing in the exquisite 'Oxford bags' (wide and floppy flannel trousers dyed in all the range of light pastel shades), in radio sets and gramophone records, in cocktail parties and the scientific study of jazz, and in the free discussion of subjects so recently taboo—sodomy, lesbianism, 'companionate marriage', and so forth. *Red Oxford*, the pamphlet history of Oxford socialism published in 1930, had nothing more serious to record of the mid-twenties than a skirmish with an excitable Vice-Chancellor, Lewis Farnell, over the right of under-graduates to express themselves freely on political matters, a controversy in which many of the senior members of the

University were most lukewarm in supporting him. As Gaitskell wrote in much later reminiscence (*Essays in Labour History*, ed. Asa Briggs, 1960), the Oxford of those days was 'gay, stimulating, and tremendously alive. The lives of the young were neither overshadowed by the consequences of the last war nor dominated by the fear of a future one'; and burgeoning then were such cultural heroes of the future as Graham Greene, Emlyn Williams, John Gielgud, John Betjeman, W. H. Auden and Cecil Day Lewis. 'The heavenly freedom of Oxford,' to quote Gaitskell again, produced 'an outburst of scepticism, a mistrust of dogma, a dislike of sentimentality and of over-emotional prejudices or violent crusades.' This was the attitude of the 'gay intellectuals' who set the tone of Oxford in those years and earned for them—and not in Oxford alone—the name of 'the roaring 'twenties'.

But this—intellectual young Oxford and the Bright Young Things of London treasure-hunt parties—was by no means all the story. To Douglas and myself, as well as to many others who had grown up in the service of the Labour movement, the war which counted, the war of poverty against wealth, of the haves against the have-nots, of the trade unions against the employing class, was by no means over. There had been, it was true, a harsh setback when the paper boom broke, and the wartime growth of working-class organisation which had produced the burgeoning of Guild Socialism, the Clyde Workers' Committee and the parallel committees of shop stewards in other industrial centres, the Building Guilds and the successful railway strike of 1919, and the ending, largely through working-class action, of the war against the Soviets (to take only a few examples), had been effectively stricken down by the crushing defeat of the miners and the Triple Alliance on Black Friday (1921) and of the Engineers in the following year. Unemployment, though not high in comparison with what it reached in later years, was already sapping trade union militancy; and the first Labour Government, brought to power by accident, by the end of 1924 had fallen flat on its back, and was not expected to be able to get up again for a long time.

Nevertheless, few of those with whom I had worked during the war were giving up the struggle or accepting the roaring 'twenties as the last word; we had merely transferred our energies to less directly political fields—such as working-class education; and when in the latter months of 1925 the Unions successfully defied the government and forced a pause in the attempt to cut miners' wages by a third or thereabouts, we felt without any astonishment that a new phase in the everlasting battle was opening. Consequently, we were excited rather than dumbfounded, when the executives of the trade unions assembled at the Memorial Hall in Farringdon Road decided with insignificant exceptions to support with the only weapon at their command the renewed attack on the miners' standard of life. To Gaitskell at Oxford, living the gay life with his contemporaries, dancing, golfing, playing bridge, working for Modern Greats, the School so recently introduced, and reading in connection therewith some, but not very much, socialist theory, the news of 3 May came as a thunderbolt.

But not, I think, a thunderbolt out of a completely clear sky. Hugh Dalton, in the volume of reminiscences entitled *Call Back Yesterday*, wrote: 'It was impossible for any generous spirit to be emotionally on the side of the masters'—the coal-owners. This is an exaggeration, the exaggeration of a Londoner already deeply committed, as we ourselves were, to the cause of the working class; not all of the thousands of university students who flocked out to join Churchill's Organisation for the Maintenance of Supplies, to drive trains and buses and unload supplies at the docks could have been called ungenerous spirits. But it *was* true of Gaitskell. Possibly his readings in socialist theory had struck deeper than he knew; at all events he discovered in a flash which side he was on, and forthwith made his way to our house in Holywell, where we had hastily formed what remained of the Oxford Labour Club into a University Strike Committee, whose purpose was to help the City Strike Committee in every possible way, by producing leaflets, by organising meetings and speakers in the town and in neighbouring villages, and by keeping in touch with London. To quote again his own words from *Essays in Labour History*:

> What could I do? Precious little. Speak at meetings? God forbid [!!]. Organize? Absolutely no experience. Had I got a car? No. Could I by any chance drive a car? Yes, I had learnt the year before. Then perhaps I could drive John Dugdale's . . . as he was taking his Schools in a few weeks he could not spare much time.

And so it happened that Hugh and I, Hugh armed with a union card from the Papermakers to get him through the London pickets, were together on that May morning, and for several mornings afterwards, on the road to London.

Even then, as I hope I have made clear, I was not thinking of Hugh particularly as a *person*—though I registered him as a pleasant and courteous companion—but rather as a promising new recruit to a cause which seemed to me as obvious as it did to Dalton. My recollection is of a competent driver, with a disconcerting speed at corners. The village of Benson in those days, before the by-pass was built, contained no fewer than nine right-angled turns, and we seemed generally to take them on two wheels, in order to avoid the risk of returning so late that Hugh would have to climb into college, with the disastrous possibility of being 'gated'. For the rest, of a rather sophisticated young man, who had seen foreign countries and could talk about the world; he seemed much more developed than my other driver, John Dugdale, though from subsequent discoveries I think I may have exaggerated and ascribed to sophistication what was simply self-control. I did not dissect him; I took him for granted, and when, as often happened, we had to hang about waiting for papers or instructions, I carted him round to call on Labour personalities. We went to the Tawneys' fearfully untidy flat in Mecklenburgh Square, where he gaped at Tawney in his old Army sergeant's jacket and washed the teacups at Jeannette Tawney's bidding; and to Clement's Inn, where in the offices of the National Maritime Board Aylmer Vallance, afterwards editor of the *News Chronicle*, who was then in a violently Red mood, spent most of his time writing fierce leaders for *Lansbury's Labour Weekly*. We conveyed personalities like the immense Will Thorne of the General Workers from Eccleston Square to the House of Commons; went to the East End through the lorries carrying TUC permits; and on the journeys to and fro, I talked to him about Labour politics and Labour personalities. What I said I cannot now remember—nor could he, in later years!—but its importance was that he was then introduced, all of a sudden, to the Labour movement as an abiding force which continued from generation to generation, and not merely as a youthful fancy for social equality which you could derive from books but which you were very likely to grow out of.

After this rather heady introduction to Labour and socialism came the next phase, in which he was Douglas's star pupil. In the autumn, having by then become a fully-fledged member of the Cole Group—which then contained many besides himself who were to play a part in the 1945 Labour Government— he decided to take 'Labour Movements' as his special subject in his Final Schools, with Douglas as his tutor. This involved frequent essays and tutorials, intensive reading and study of the lives and character of dead-and-gone leaders, and led to one of his few published works, a little history of Chartism. After Douglas's death, Hugh paid eloquent tribute to the 'wonderfully stimulating quality' of these tutorials, to the new and exciting world which they opened for him, to the sense Douglas gave him of being treated as completely adult—'a research worker rather than someone to be pushed through an examination'—and the total absence of any *de haut-en-bas* attitude, of any desire, despite his own strong convictions, to play the part of 'a prophet with a message'. Douglas, for his part, appreciated his star pupil for three main reasons. First, because of his command of English—a quality still, alas, not over-common among economists. Douglas more than once told me that Gaitskell was the only pupil of his who could write decently. Secondly, because he was a young man with a background of culture, who could share—or could be induced to share—his tutor's wide interests in literature, fine glass, and in the English countryside. (One of the minor debts which Hugh acknowledged was being taught how to find pleasure and social history in walking with his tutor through the lanes and fields and woods of Cobbett's country in southern England.) And thirdly, because Hugh was both of great intellectual ability and tough-minded, and used the 'equality of treatment' of which he spoke so often to argue with his mentor, and occasionally to convince him. I doubt whether Hugh was ever a natural hero-worshipper; but certainly his own independence of mind was fostered by being in early contact with a man who had little use for acolytes.

He did not remain *in statu pupillari* for long; in 1927 he got his First in Schools. But in the next stage (which he again called 'a turning-point in my life') the influence of Douglas was decisive. When he was trying to decide which, of the careers that lay open to an Oxford First, he should try to pursue, Douglas dined him in Soho, and made *inter alia* the suggestion that, if he had any inclination towards adult education, he should try for the job of tutor for extra-mural classes in Nottingham; he elected to do so, and on Douglas's recommendation was appointed.

Though he stayed only for a year in Nottingham, after which he obtained a teaching post in University College,

London, the Nottingham interlude is of great importance for the understanding of Hugh's development, for two reasons. First, the fact that, with a good many more lucrative possibilities open to him he chose 'with tremendous pleasure' (his own words) to start in the field of adult education, which was then —as to some extent it still is—the Cinderella of the academic world in both payment and prospects, showed clearly that the conversion of the year before was a real one and not a passing emotion of generosity; the purpose of his life was fairly fixed. But secondly, and much more important, it provided him with the only actual contact he had for many years with the individual, *working* members of the working class whose leader he was to become. Up to that time, though he had met many intellectuals devoted to the working-class cause—and a few union officials—he had scarcely set eyes, effectively, on an authentic working man—a deficiency which did not apply to Attlee, with his Army experience and his long residence among the dockers of Stepney. Short as it was, the experience made an immense impression on Hugh. I well remember his talking to me, more than once, of the shock he received in discovering, through some of his class students, the real conditions of life in the coalfields—and it will be recollected that Nottingham had suffered far less than some other districts by the end of the long strike—and telling me of the occasion when he asked a Nottingham street-walker what her charges were and received the reply, 'Fourpence, dearie—*or sixpence if it's in the cemetery.*'

For that year, of course, we lost close contact with Hugh; but when he moved to London, and both of us were still taking weekly tutorial classes for London University, we helped out his finances, by hiring as a *pied-à-terre* a room in the flat he had rented in a rather dilapidated Georgian house at the less refined end of Great Ormond Street. Before that, we had been living in a flat by Regent's Park belonging to another tutor, Amyas Ross, who now required the room for his own use.

I am very conscious that, largely owing to constrictions of space, the preceding pages have tended to give an impression of Hugh Gaitskell as a kind of young St. Paul, who while living a life of fun and frivolity at Oxford saw the vision of Damascus on the Henley road, and thereafter abjured all his earlier pastimes. This would not be at all correct, even though his friendship with Evan Durbin seemed in part to bear it out. Evan, Hugh's contemporary at New College and his lifelong friend, was a person of austere mind as well as great kindness of heart. When I first knew him, he gave an appearance of truculent morality—perhaps because he was originally intended to be a preacher—and of wanting to damn all who strayed from a path beaten by his own convictions; and though he mellowed very thoroughly in his later years, for a long time outsiders received the impression, rightly or wrongly, that Evan was Hugh's conscience and pulled him sharply back whenever he showed signs of deviating into light-mindedness. But though the General Strike did produce a conversion in Hugh—or rather, perhaps, greatly accelerated a conversion which was already beginning—it was not devastating; it did not change him into a different sort of person. He still enjoyed (as to the end of his life he enjoyed) dancing, games, food and drink, and the normal pleasures of society; and it was this, as well as a coincidence of occupation, which brought him into the position of collaborator with—and in part financier of— Amyas and Peggy Ross in the Soho Gallery, a concern engaged in the distribution of prints and reproductions of paintings.

Amyas Ross, who died at forty as the result of a car accident, was one of the oddest characters ever to appear in so respectable an organisation as the adult education movement. Remarkably good-looking, and with many outstanding gifts, particularly for musical improvisation, he had become a violent socialist when very young, to the horror of his kind conventional parents—I remember him as a schoolboy turning up in

the offices of the Labour Research Department in 1917 demand-
ing on behalf of the sixth form at Repton School instructions
on what they could do to help on the social revolution. No one
who knew Amyas will ever forget him—his energy, his
eagerness, his many ideas, some fruitful, some fantastic—or his
unique ability to get himself and his surroundings into a mess,
both physically and in every other possible way. From arriving
to take a class unshaven, dressed in dirty flannels and a dress
shirt, because the gas had been cut off for non-payment, and
all his normal shirts were lying in his bath awaiting hot water,
to becoming involved emotionally with several women
simultaneously and being unable to break the date which he
did not want to keep because he had no money in his pocket
and could not succeed in cadging the twopence for a telephone
call, or to making up a paper which he edited by covering a
bouncing railway carriage with galleys, scissors and a corkless
bottle of gum while listening to music on a portable gramophone—he was by turns an exasperation and a stimulus to all
his friends, one of whom was Hugh Gaitskell. Hugh (whom
the Rosses always addressed as 'Sam', for what reason I now
forget), having a little money of his own to spare, became
chairman of the then rickety company in its hand-to-mouth,
day-to-day existence; and I think found considerable if not
unadulterated pleasure in following its fortunes and the very
bohemian preoccupations of its principal founder (it subsequently got well on its feet, and is still flourishing); and this
helped to save him from a 'superior' attitude which might
have resulted from socialist convictions combined with intellectual distinction.

At any rate it was a variant on learning up banking and
currency—subjects which he had not studied at Oxford—in
order to persuade out-of-work miners to want to take classes
in them—and the same is true of Hugh's acquaintance with
the Mitchisons, G. R. and Naomi, which also came about

towards the end of the decade. Naomi took a great initial fancy
to him, and I have clear recollections of him at the Mitchisons'
parties in Hammersmith and the house-parties which they
collected in Scottish baronial castles, enjoying very much the
talk and the miscellaneous collection of 'radicals' of all kinds
and occupations who gathered there—even if he did once
write indignantly to me, 'I *will not* be a character in one of
Naomi's novels'. Rôle-playing, to use modern jargon, was not
his idea of pleasure, though he liked house-party games and
charades, and once appeared as a Roman emperor in a bath-
towel—he managed to look remarkably dissolute.

Most of these 'interludes' took place after the foundation of
the Socialist Society for Information and Propaganda and the
New Fabian Research Bureau, in which he played a prominent
part. I have described the creation of these bodies in my
Story of Fabian Socialism, and do not propose to repeat myself
here; but in order to get the picture clear it is necessary to recall
that in 1930, when it was becoming manifest that the Labour
Government which followed the 1929 election (in which Hugh
had blooded himself for the first time in Labour politics) was
being no more of an inspiration than its predecessor, Douglas
and I, with two or three collaborators, launched, at a series of
week-end conferences held in Easton Lodge, the Essex home
of Lady Warwick, whose tenant nearby was H. G. Wells, a
project which we hoped would both rekindle fervour in the
Labour movement and start the practical thinking, of which so
little had been done in the 'twenties, of what a Labour Government in power really ought to try and do.

For a movement started with no finances at all, and with
recruitment done at first entirely by individual personal appeal,
this venture of ours went ahead remarkably fast. The strictly
propaganda side of it (SSIP), unfortunately, made the mistake
of merging itself with the anti-Maxton branch of the ILP to
form the short-lived Socialist League, which itself perished in

following Maxton's bad example by trying to establish, while *inside* the Labour Party, an alternative policy to that of the leadership, and was promptly treated as Maxton had been; NFRB, on the contrary, forcing no conformity on its membership, went ahead steadily, eventually taking over the moribund Fabian Society and making it into the institution which it is today.

Gaitskell, in the essay already quoted, paid a handsome tribute to the influence and importance of the New Fabian Research Bureau; and he should know, for he was very closely connected with its foundation. Our personal appeal was naturally directed to all of those whom we had known in previous enterprises, who might be disillusioned with MacDonald's government—and how many of these there were, after only eighteen months of experience and before the mass unemployment had shown it up fully, let apologists for MacDonald remember. And among these, naturally, a fertile field was expected to be the members and ex-members of the Cole Group in Oxford, who were young, with some spare time on their hands (since no one, then, thought of marrying in his student days!) and who had, moreover, in their weekly sessions been endeavouring in some measure to do what NFRB was now proposing on a national and more professional scale. Contemporaries of Hugh at Oxford, E. A. Radice and John Parker (now MP for Dagenham), became successively the secretaries of the new organization, and Hugh himself its assistant honorary secretary, with G. D. H. Cole as his immediate superior.

From the first he showed exactly the qualities I should have expected him to show. Douglas made him secretary of the Bureau's Economic Section, for whose work he had provided, as was his wont, an enormous programme running to over a dozen typed foolscap pages. Hugh, then working in University College, tackled this without a murmur of hesitation, was nearly, if not quite, as effective as his chief in the matter of running committees, minuting them and preparing drafts. By 1933 (the Bureau having been effectively established in the spring of 1931) the Economic Section had spawned no fewer than eleven sub-committees, all of which were reported to be 'working well'. Not having been a member of any of these, I cannot confirm this statement from personal experience. But from my knowledge of the two of them I do not find it at all difficult to credit; and the tale of NFRB's published work on economic subjects, taken together with the more specialized memoranda which remained unpublished but available for consultation in its files, goes far to bear it out.

Gaitskell edited, for a while, the rather over-imposing *Quarterly Journal* of the Bureau, which after a while was reduced, for financial reasons—*all* 'progressive' organizations tend to overspending—to something about half the size and more general in its appeal. He was not by any means the Bureau's only professional economist. Besides Evan Durbin, names like those of Colin Clark, Gilbert Walker, J. E. Meade, E. F. Schumacher, E. V. Nash, Erich Roll and others of subsequent distinction are to be found in its early records; but certainly he, partly but not by any means entirely because of his close relations with its founder, played very much of a leading part. I am not sure whether it was at that time that he came under the notice of Hugh Dalton, who was one of the earliest sponsors of the Bureau at a dinner in the House of Commons, held with the expressed goodwill of Sidney and Beatrice Webb, still the leaders of the Fabian Society, and of Arthur Henderson, then Secretary of the Party. Their meeting may have taken place earlier—even while Hugh was still at Oxford, for one of Dalton's most valuable traits was his deep interest in young socialists and his flair for spotting winners at the embryonic stage; it is certain, however, that by 1933 Dalton must have had him in his eye—a factor of great importance for his career in the years which fall outside the scope of this chapter. (Much earlier, almost at the outset of his time in Oxford, the younger Hugh had appealed to his future chief, Stafford Cripps, as a fellow Wykehamist, for guidance; as, however, Stafford was at the moment in a very great hurry and could only tell him, in a short interview in a taxi, that what the Labour movement principally needed was a re-orientation on Christian principles, an idea which made little appeal to Hugh, this contact proved of small immediate value to him.)

With all this intellectual activity going on at such a pace, it is not surprising that the crash of the Labour Government in 1931 caused comparatively little consternation among the NFRB enthusiasts, who had already in their minds written off MacDonald and his principal colleagues as hopeless from the socialist point of view. Rather, they tended to go on with their chosen work as though nothing much had happened; and though the election which followed was far more catastrophic than anybody had imagined until the first results were announced over the radio, its effect on them was stimulating rather than numbing. 'What did we tell you?' was the feeling. '*Now* let us really get down to earth, and work out and present to the Labour Party the kind of programme which will bring back a real socialist government with a majority.' The membership of NFRB began to rise significantly, its conferences and pamphlets to receive more serious attention, and the job of the secretary of the Economic Section to increase. (It was less than a year after the election that, with Hugh's support, it cut itself free from its SSIP partner.)

Hugh did not take part in the Bureau's first major venture, the team of investigators which in the summer of 1932 it sent to the USSR in the wake of the Webbs—possibly because he found the not inconsiderable cost of the tour more than he wanted to incur, possibly for other reasons. It was certainly not from any lack of sympathy with the object of study. It must not be forgotten that in 1932, when the world depression was reaching its height, the Nazis striding to power in Germany, the Disarmament Conference dragging patently to its end, and British Labour ingloriously collapsed, it was generally assumed that real socialists must be both profoundly interested in and sympathetic towards the Socialist Sixth of the World. It was not essential to fall in love with the USSR like the authors of *Soviet Communism*; but it was natural to be on the side of the Russians, and people like Evan Durbin, who almost from the first hated the Soviet leaders as oppressors and deniers of the human rights of individuals, were apt to be regarded as shocking reactionaries. The fact that Hugh accepted and supported the Russians does not mean that he was ever on the extreme Left. I should myself have described him at that time as of the centre—but as more interested, on the whole, in practical problems, in making things work, than in dogma either Right or Left. It is perhaps symptomatic that when he was adopted as candidate for Chatham in 1932, he happily spoke on platforms with avowed communists until his local party told him he must not—when he accepted the ban without protest. He was, perhaps, a bit of a desk—not an armchair—politician in a situation which was certainly not revolutionary; until early in 1934 a change of scene brought him sharply up against the realities of politics in Europe.

He had seized upon a chance to go to Vienna with a Rockefeller grant in order to study some questions of economic theory. The nature of the assignment, however, is of little importance, because as soon as he got there he fell in love with the Red Vienna which some of us still remember, with its fine workers' flats and its gay young socialist directors—and within a very short time had his first taste of fascism in action, with Dolfuss's *Heimwehr* beating down the working-class associations, cannonading the Karl Marx Hof, and hanging Koloman

Wallisch in the best Nazi tradition. He was at a party of Vienna socialists on the February night when the civil war broke out, and the machine-guns were firing in the streets as he went home. At once he went into action and set about doing what he could to help. To us in Hendon there came an urgent appeal to raise money to help with relief for the victims, and above all to tell everyone in Britain what was happening in Austria. The appeal was followed by a tall young Austrian economist, passing under the name of Rudolf Gessner, whom we sent around the country speaking. In response to Hugh we raised all the funds we could, tried to wake up the slow-moving Socialist International and alerted the *Manchester Guardian* and other journals. Naomi Mitchison went out to Vienna to help 'Sam'; in the *Vienna Diary* she later published a vivid account of the defeat of the socialists. Elwyn Jones, the lawyer who is now MP for West Ham, came out to aid the defence, and Citrine of the TUC on behalf of the trade unions.

The fight against fascism failed, as it had already failed in Germany and was to fail in Spain; but it had given Hugh a new outlook and an increased stature. The intense work of organization and improvisation which he performed during those few weeks showed him his own ability, and displayed it, also, to persons like Citrine who were high in Labour counsels; and his sight of guns in action had convinced him that the rising tide of oppression was not to be driven back by traditional pacifist policies. When he came back to England he was already set to try and convince the Labour Party of the need for getting arms against the dictatorship, and he was ripe to take an increasing part in policy-making in the Labour Party. This meant that though our acquaintance did not cease, the special relationship born of the General Strike, his association with Douglas, and the New Fabian Research Bureau came gradually to an end. He was on his way into politics; and here I must leave his career to others.

POLITICAL AND INTELLECTUAL PROGRESS

Michael Postan

The fifteen or sixteen years between 1930 and 1945 saw important changes in Hugh Gaitskell's personal circumstances: his coming to London, his academic post at University College, his involvement with party work, his earliest election campaign, his year of study and socialist rising in Vienna, his entry into Government service with the outbreak of war, his friendship and collaboration with Hugh Dalton, and, over-laying all this, his marriage. I propose to confine myself to what I know of his political and intellectual progress in this period. We were close friends, constantly in each other's company, more especially in the years between 1929 and 1934 when I lived in London, and again between 1939 and 1943 when we both worked in the Ministry of Economic Warfare and lived in Eileen Power's and my house in Mecklenburgh Square. Moreover, our friendship was exceedingly socratic and even didactic. We argued incessantly and incontinently all the time we were together, even on walking holidays in the Lakes or at dancing parties at the Gargoyle. As a result we came to know or to believe we knew one another's ideas almost as well as our own.

I knew Hugh Gaitskell slightly in his Nottingham years. We had met once in a WEA class on the Industrial Revolution, which he was conducting, and again a few months later during his visit to London at a party given by John Gray, then a young sociologist at LSE. Such, however, was my lack of perception that I did not carry away a clear or a true impression of Hugh as a person. In Nottingham he struck me as one of the typical Oxbridge left-wingers who were a drug on the market in those days. At a London party we conversed for a while, but to me he appeared merely as another of the well-spoken Bloomsburyites of the second generation—Nineteen-Seventeen-Club, Cave of Harmony and all that.

I came to realize how mistaken I was a year later when circumstances brought us closely together. We were both junior lecturers at University College, and towards the end of the first term of 1930 we found ourselves sitting opposite each other at the annual dinner of the Professorial Dining Club. The occasion was very convivial and wine was both good and plentiful; so when we found ourselves alone he turned to me with a question much more direct than one he would have allowed himself on a more sober occasion. 'I see you are not a fool, but I am told you hold *émigré* views about Russia: how can you?' And thus started the first of the many, indeed hundreds of dialogues between us on politics, social philosophy, socialism, Russia, economics, methodology. In this very first dialogue Hugh already was fully the man he was to show himself in intimate debate throughout the years that followed: an ideal listener, attentive and courteous, full of respect for his collocutor and anxious to meet him most of the way, yet too concerned in the subject matter and too firm in his own views ever to pretend to agree for mere politeness or to retreat beyond the main line of his defence.

Within less than a year of this first encounter Evan Durbin, an Oxford friend of Hugh's and another recent recruit to University College, joined us in the conversations. By 1930 they had already arrived at a mutual understanding which for newcomers like myself was, to begin with, almost impenetrable. They were, of course, too different as persons to agree on every subject. Evan Durbin was already set in his views, which were essentially those he was to hold for the rest of his life, whereas Hugh Gaitskell was still very much on the move. The touch of finality in Durbin's convictions was of immense value to Hugh who came to rely upon the assured, down-to-earth, good sense which Evan appeared to ooze out of every pore. Hugh would often take from Evan propositions which he might decline when offered by others, and it often fell to Evan to act as a broker between Hugh and me.

Our triangle was by no means self-sufficient. Hugh's ideas and interests in psychology (in common with most of his contemporaries he was for a time a convinced Freudian) were served by another friend of Evan Durbin's, John Bowlby. On rare but immensely important occasions we had R. H. Tawney with us. He had got to know Hugh and Evan through Eileen Power and myself, and developed a great liking for them. But needless to say our encounters with Tawney never took the form of ordinary discussions. In his company we were prepared to sit and listen, amused by the wit and aptness of his language and enraptured by the image of the man himself, to us the greatest living Englishman. The views he held happened to be very near those to which Hugh was moving by himself, but from Tawney's conversation they always emerged washed clean of all triviality and glowing with his philosophy and poetry.

From 1931 onwards, more especially in the war years when Hugh came to live with us, most of our encounters and discussions took place in Eileen Power's presence, usually at our house in Mecklenburgh Square. I believe it was she who brought Gaitskell and Durbin to Dalton's notice. I was present at the dinner party in 1930 to which Dalton and Tawney were invited by Eileen to meet them; and I remember having to defend ourselves, after Hugh and Evan had gone, against Dalton's accusation of 'hoarding' for our exclusive use these 'charming young socialists'.

Some of our discussions took place in gatherings which were relatively large and formally constituted. One such series of gatherings was organized by Hugh and Evan in 1931 to discuss the economics of socialist society. The early meetings of the group were in the basement of Bogey's Bar, a café which John Bowlby and Durbin ran for several years in the building of the Royal Hotel. The first meeting was heavily weighted by young economists of whom James Meade was one; surprisingly enough Roy Harrod also attended on one or two occasions. As the 'thirties advanced, the meetings were transferred to the London School of Economics and became somewhat less formal.

These meetings petered out in the early years of the war, but one of these war-time gatherings which may or may not have been a part of the series stands out very clearly in my memory. It was a largely informal encounter in my flat in 1943 with George Woodcock, now Secretary of the TUC, What we discussed was the place of the professional *élite* in socialist movements. Woodcock remained highly sceptical and poured scorn on the evanescent socialism of young middle-class intellectuals. This resistance of Woodcock's apparently greatly impressed Hugh who confided to me on the following day his fear that it would take a long time to wean English socialists away from the traditional identification of socialism with the industrial proletariat. 'They will be shocked, and they will call us fascists.'

Wholly different, more academic in purpose and composition, was the group which Eileen Power and myself, with Hugh's encouragement, formed in 1932 to discuss the sociological and historical implications of economic problems. The list of papers presented to the group which I still possess contains the names, in addition to our own, of Walter Adams (now Vice-Chancellor in the University of Southern Rhodesia), T. H. Marshall, D. W. Brogan, and John Hawgood (now Professor of History in Birmingham).

More infrequent but nevertheless quite significant for Hugh's political development were our attendances at *Tots and Quots*. This was a dining club formed by G. P. (Gip) Wells and Solly Zuckerman, which met on Saturday nights in *Quo Vadis*, a Soho restaurant, to discuss scientific method. I always suspected that the original inspiration behind the dinners was Gip Well's liking for good food in congenial company, but the official purpose was to expound the unity of scientific method in all fields of enquiry, political and economic as well as purely scientific. In those days the phrase 'unity of scientific method' had a distinct Marxist ring. The intention of the founders was to assemble men of many specialities and of every shade of opinion (*tot homines, quot opiniones*), but the attendance and the ideas were largely provided by the Marxist or near-Marxist scientists. 'Sage' Bernal was frequently there and was as always forceful and prolific. I came very infrequently and read a paper only once, but Hugh came more often, partly for the sake of the wine and the food, but mainly because he was at that time passing through a phase in which Marxists and their talk drew him irresistibly by the very provocation they caused. Such anti-Marxist predispositions as he already had were strengthened by what he heard and discussed at *Quo Vadis*.

These various groups and encounters formed the background to Hugh's intellectual life in the 'thirties or rather to that side of his life in which I participated. It goes without saying that his universe was much wider. He was after all a serious, indeed a dedicated, economist, and was also increasingly drawn into the political and administrative activities of the Labour Party. He knew well all the economists at LSE (for a time in Oxford he had been Lionel Robbins's pupil), and was very friendly with both N. Kaldor and Thomas Balogh. However, the economist with whom he was most intimate was his colleague at University College, Paul Rosenstein Rodan, a man of immense erudition, ingenuity, and generosity, who greatly contributed to Hugh's development as an economist.

Finally, there were the miscellaneous friendships which Hugh formed so easily and maintained so firmly. Some dated from his Winchester and Oxford days and even his days at the Dragon School. Among these friendships which were to mature and deepen in London was that with Frank Pakenham, who at one time shared rooms with him in Oxford, and with his wife Elizabeth. Different again was another Oxford friendship which Hugh shared with Evan—that of John MacMurray, who inspired them in Oxford as a teacher of philosophy but who soon became a colleague and a close friend at UCL. Hugh also spoke of Maurice Bowra as one of his most rewarding Oxford friendships, and of John Betjeman, whom he had known at Dragons and in Oxford.

His Bloomsbury contacts also ripened into a large number of friendships which I cannot enumerate here. Two of these friendships I must, however, single out—that with the Mitchisons and that with Amyas Ross. For a period in 1932 the Mitchison household in Hammersmith provided him with a stimulating and varied company of left-wing intellectuals, and for this and other reasons was for a time something of a magnet. On the other hand Amyas Ross, a gentle and feckless waif, one of Bloomsbury's earliest beatniks, was a source of constant preoccupation. Hugh, together with another friend, founded the Soho Gallery, sellers and publishers of modern reproductions, mainly in order to provide Ross with an occupation. In the war Hugh got Dalton to give Ross employment in the Ministry of Economic Warfare and even persuaded Ross to put on a dark suit and to keep office hours. Those who know Hugh can easily imagine his distress when a few months later Ross was found dead in his sordid little apartment off New Oxford Street—dead from neglect after a 'flu. Overshadowing all these personal contacts and friendships were his emotional links with his elder brother Arthur, whose infrequent visits to London on leave from Sudan were times of great upheaval; and of course his link with his wife. Few people know and only Hugh himself could have recounted all that Dora meant and did for him in those years—the care she lavished on him when he needed it most, the understanding and stimulus he found in her company. And Hugh alone knew how much he owed to her advice and to her steady and persistent influence.

At the time of our earliest discussions—in 1929 and 1930—Hugh Gaitskell's socialist convictions appeared at first sight to be of the typical inter-war Oxbridge variety. They were couched in a language which was nothing if not radical. The words 'class war', 'social revolution', and 'proletariat' rolled off his tongue easily and smoothly, and the words 'intellectual' and 'middle-class' he used as often as not as terms of opprobrium. He was perhaps already too much of an economist to speak glibly of capitalist exploitation and wage slavery, but the memories of the General Strike and the coal strike and his personal experiences of working-class life in Nottinghamshire had bitten deeply into him. He thought of poverty, inequality, unemployment and slums with emotion and spoke of them with heat. I do not remember his using in private discussion the formula of 'common ownership of the means of production', but I do not think it occurred to him at that time to question nationalization of industry as the crowning object of socialism. In spite of all his doubts about the Soviet Union he still spoke of it as 'the great socialist country' and blamed the faults of the Soviet régime on the Russian national character.

To us in the earliest 'thirties all this was familiar stuff: the typical assortment of ideas most young socialists held at the time. Yet what struck me at our very first conversation at the Professorial Dinner Club was the note of doubt he sounded every

time he brought out a stock idea. This condition of incipient
heterodoxy may have come from having been previously
treated to G. D. H. Cole's unorthodox variants of socialism.
But in Hugh's case many of the doubts were of too recent an
origin to be traceable to Cole. They bore the mark of 1930,
and they grew from year to year in the subsequent decade.

Contrary to the 'rightist' image which Hugh acquired in
later years the one aspect of Hugh's socialism which appeared
to me to change least in the 'thirties and early 'forties was its
radicalism. Until 1945 (and our contacts after that date became
too infrequent for me to be able to judge) Hugh preserved
almost intact his emotional predilection for radical solutions.
Again, contrary to his public image of later years he was
by temperament, or rather by logic, a whole-hogger. This
showed itself in his policy in MEW on blockade and neutral
rights; in the influence he had on the 1949 devaluation, more
drastic than that favoured by many of his colleagues; in the
manner in which he chose to present his opposition to Clause
4, and in his final attitude to the Common Market. On all these
occasions he was of course concerned with immediate political
issues, not with final socialist objectives, but those who know him
best would probably agree that both before and after 1945 the
vision of equality which inspired his socialism was more intense
and more far-reaching than that of most Labour politicians.
Where he changed most in the 'thirties was not so much in the
intensity of his views as in their contents, i.e. not in their quantity
but in their essence: in the intellectual make-up of his socialist
ideal.

To my mind (the scale of priorities is entirely my own) the
most fundamental of these changes was his gradual abandonment of the proletarian sociology of socialism. In the end, i.e.
by 1945, his views on class demarcations and on the alignment
of interests for and against socialism came to resemble the
views which historians of socialism would recognize as

'populist'. When we first met he was writing, or had just finished writing, an essay on the Chartists, and the question which bothered him most was the social make-up of the Chartist movement. How was it, he asked, that the advocates of revolutionary action and the early socialists found their following not so much among the rising class of industrial proletariat as among the *déclassé* victims of the Industrial Revolution, mainly refugees from petit bourgeois occupations?

These doubts prepared the ground for the continued discussions of this problem in the following decade. In 1931 and 1932 I devoted a large part of my course on the economic history of great powers at LSE to the recent trends in the social structure of industrial employment and above all to the proliferation of the various *élites* and the relative decline in the semi-skilled employments. Evan Durbin who attended the course suggested that we might try to work out the implications of this trend for socialist policy. These implications had already come up in discussions between Hugh and me, and it is therefore not surprising that they should have occupied us at a number of the earliest meetings in Bogey's Bar. In the end Durbin incorporated his and our ideas on this subject into his *Politics of Democratic Socialism*. On his part Hugh gradually made up his mind that the whole conception of socialism would have to be fitted to a future wherein the personnel of industry and the political following of popular parties would be composed of those very elements whom the *Communist Manifesto* dismissed as the fellow-travellers of the bourgeoisie. This topic preoccupied Hugh during a memorable week-end he spent with me in Cambridge in 1936, and this was also the topic which he repeatedly brought up at the gatherings of Eileen Power's sociological group. If on my return to London in 1939 the subject no longer entered into our conversation with any frequency, this was mainly because Durbin's book was already completed and Hugh's views on the subject

appeared to be fully formed. Woodcock's reaction to my
somewhat extreme exposition of the idea disturbed Hugh,
precisely because it boded ill for future chances of transmuting
the social appeal of socialism.

Hugh's views on the sociology of socialism developed
concurrently with his views of nationalization. I do not know
how far the ethos of Cole's 'guild socialism' or of Tawney's
Acquisitive Society were responsible for his earliest doubts about
nationalization as the only way of conducting industry in a
socialist society. Evan, in his empirical fashion, insisted on
discussing the virtues and vices of nationalization not as an
ideal and not in global terms but pragmatically, industry by
industry. This we frequently did at the meetings at Bogey's
Bar. On my own part I pressed on Hugh my conviction that
all-embracing state ownership, as in Soviet Russia, was
compatible with a society more inimical to the real purposes
of socialism than even Baldwin's England. In addition Hugh
and Evan were drawn into the debate on socialist planning and
pricing systems which proceeded all through the 'thirties among
the younger LSE economists and in which for a time Abraham
Lerner and Paul Sweezy (both at that time near-communists)
were most active. From this debate we all emerged with the
conviction that the economic purposes of socialism could be attained by properly inspired and properly conducted central planning, and that for a socialist transformation of the economy
the 'command of the strategic heights' (a typical pre-war formula!) would suffice.

My impression, however, is that all these influences provided
the make-weight, not the mainspring, of Hugh's evolution.
He was moving and would have moved in this direction by
his own momentum. For to him the essence of socialism always
was equality and social justice; and, as far as I can remember,
he always declared himself to be uncommitted to the choice
of means. When he came to consider practical proposals for

individual industries or for land he invariably turned out to be more radical than Evan or some of his other friends. I also know from some of our infrequent discussions in the late 'fifties that, had he been then in power, his shopping list of industries and interests to be nationalized would have been far wider than that of many of the defenders of Clause 4. He was not, however, prepared to identify socialism with nationalization of industry; and to this view he had come to be firmly wedded by 1939 at the very latest.

These views of socialist purposes, class alignments, and common ownership were of course highly un-Marxist. When I first met him his conversation was still larded with Marxian phraseology and he still found amusement in jokes about my 'anti-Marxist prejudice'. Like all economists of that time, he rejected the labour theory of value and dismissed as beside the point the whole Marxist economic theory, including his theory of crises (Joan Robinson's preoccupations with Vols. II and III of *Das Kapital* came more than a decade later). But while rejecting Marxian economics he took it for granted that Marxian sociology and economic history still held good and were proper intellectual tools for a socialist to employ.

Yet even at that time his Marxian attachments were very fragile. I have already mentioned his early doubts about Marxist class analysis, and I soon discovered that his general outlook was not materialist and certainly not dialectical. Dialectics were to him the most unpalatable ingredient of Marxian philosophy. The dialectical jargon current among his contemporaries—the 'negation of the negation', 'the transmutation of quantity into quality' and all the rest of it—were wholly alien to his mode of speaking and thinking. One night in 1934 on our walk through Soho after a long session with a certain communist professor, Hugh proclaimed—somewhat angrily as if the fault were mine—that he found the whole system of dialectical notions hollow and boring. To please me he had struggled through the *Anti-Dühring* and blamed me for it ever after. In fact in spite of my anti-Marxist views I often found myself acting as an *advocatus diaboli* trying to commend to Hugh the subtleties of Marxian exegesis. But in general he preferred to hear the ideology expounded and defended by those who believed in it. This may have been one of the uses to which he put his encounters with the Marxists at the *Tots and Quots*.

On another nocturnal walk home after a meeting at which I read a paper on class conflicts he inveighed against the self-contained logic of the dialectic. When I replied that it was no more self-contained than the logic of marginal economics or of Freudian psychology, he came back with strictures on the individual propositions of Marxian ideology and especially on the proposition that evolution proceeded by conflicts of opposites, or that significant class demarcations were always determined by social relations of production, or that the economic factor was at the base of social phenomena, or that there was a meaningful distinction between 'base' and 'super-structure'. In his frequent conversational inquests on the Austro-German social democrats he invariably spoke of their Marxism as one of their afflictions.

This, I believe, became his settled opinion some time before the war. In 1935 I sent him from Cambridge a reprint of an essay on Marx, which I had contributed to Barrett Brown's *Great Democrats*, and he wrote back to say that the whole world of Marxist ideas was now so remote from his real preoccupations that he had lost all interest in it and that it was about time I did likewise.

His views on Russia were not influenced by his revulsion from Marxism, but they nevertheless moved in the same direction. His youthful notions about Russia as a great social-istic experiment and about the temporary and self-healing character of the Soviet dictatorship did not survive for very long. My own stories and views may have contributed to his disillusionments, and so did also his contacts with continental social democrats. He read widely into the current literature about the USSR, but distrusted much of what he read and strongly reacted against the tales brought back by the returning hordes of 'intourists'. On the other hand he met through me a number of Western experts who had served the Soviet régime or spent some time in Russia on specialist assignments. The report which I believe had the greatest effect on him was that of the well-known Canadian agricultural adviser, Cairns, who had made an extended study of Stalin's collectivization and whom I saw a great deal on his way back from Russia. Stalin's régime with its accumulation of lies and horrors had of course the same effect on Hugh as it had on other socialists in the 1930s; and when the war broke out his position in the intelligence branch of MEW enabled him to see a great deal of information which confirmed his worst views of Stalin's régime. He had been among the very few of my friends who were neither surprised nor unduly shocked by the Molotov-Ribbentrop agreement.

Yet it is curious how inconspicuous Hugh Gaitskell's attitude to Russia remained. During the war the Russian section of MEW was one of my responsibilities, and we in the Ministry not only formed an optimistic view of Russia's capacity to withstand the German invasion, but also took the initiative in organizing the economic assistance to Russia. The Ministry therefore acquired in some Government circles the reputation of being specially pro-Russian, and of reflecting thereby the socialist sympathies of Dalton and Gaitskell. Only Hugh's friends knew how far apart even at that time were Hugh's sympathies from his judgement of political and military realities.

His attitudes to the Soviet régime and still more his attitude to Nazi Germany reflected not only his political views but also his own brand of Englishry. He was deeply English in most things, including his political attitudes; and by degrees these attitudes became sufficiently conscious to become a subject of debate between him, Evan Durbin and myself. Needless to say, Hugh's nationalism was entirely a matter of loyalties and allegiances and was utterly devoid of any phobias. He had numerous foreign friends and easily associated with foreigners in England and abroad. In recent years several prominent socialists abroad confessed to me that they found him the most congenial of the English Labour leaders. These sympathies went together with his liking for foreign travel. In this respect he was very unlike Durbin who was never happy away from England and preferred Cotswolds and Cornwall to all other holiday playgrounds. Yet although Gaitskell used to chide Durbin for his insularity, he invariably placed his own socialist ideas and his visions of the future in a purely English setting. In one of our conversations with Tawney in 1933 we got him to describe his social work in the slums of pre-1914 Manchester, and heard him say that all through that time he felt humiliated by the sight of 'his fellow Englishmen' in their abject condition. Later, when left alone with Hugh, I commented on the words used—fellow Englishmen, not fellow human beings—but Hugh, after a brief pause, confessed that he would have used the same words. He had reasoned himself into international socialism, but his vision of the future was one of England's Jerusalem. During his sojourn in Vienna he soon established contacts with the local party, formed close personal links with one or two individuals and was drawn into the actual business of the Socialist risings. But on the whole his residence abroad brought home to him his Englishness, his dependence on the English milieu, and his preference for English ways. On the day of his return to London, Eileen Power and I met him at the Russell Square Underground and took him out for a meal to a grill room in Southampton Row. Once inside, he eagerly sniffed the air and his face lit up. 'English sausages, how much I missed them in Vienna!' And over a plate of bacon and sausages he told us how much the minutiae of English life meant to him, how conscious he was abroad of being an Englishman and how good it was to be coming home.

At first sight these manifestations of his Englishry may have appeared purely superficial, but in the course of the following two or three years their deeper roots worked their way to the surface. Hugh was a determined and clear-cut anti-Munichite: an attitude which endeared him to Hugh Dalton, but for a time brought him into conflict with Evan Durbin. He moved fast to a belief in the inevitability or indeed the necessity of war with Hitler—a war that would not only rescue the world from a dreadful tyranny, but save the independence and the integrity of England. His attitude was probably more uncompromising than that of any other of the Labour men I knew, except perhaps Hugh Dalton. In the spring of 1939 we all attended a Labour Conference in the Garden House Hotel at Cambridge devoted to the discussion of the international situation. Stafford Cripps, assisted by Konni Zilliacus, urged the socialists to resist the preparations for war. In a speech remarkable for its closely argued *non-sequitors* Cripps took the line that of the two evils, imperialism and fascism, imperialism was the more abhorrent, and that a successful war against Hitler would, while destroying fascism, strengthen British imperialism. Sentiments like these when uttered by Zilliacus were not of course taken seriously. Coming from Cripps and delivered with the cold ruthlessness of a hanging judge they were bound to shock all of us, even Evan Durbin, very profoundly. After the conference Douglas Jay drove Hugh and some of us to London, and in his crowded car we all studiously avoided all reference to Cripps. It was not until we had got to London that Hugh laughingly and angrily—a characteristic mixture—gave vent to his feelings about Cripps and the coming crisis.

Hugh worked and slaved during the war in MEW and

later in the Board of Trade with a concentration, indeed a dedication, which I did not find at all surprising, but he did not expose the springs of his war activity in my company, except once, and once only. One night in early December 1940, during the second or the third of the great night raids on London, German bombs fell on Caroline Place and on two houses in Mecklenburgh Square not far from us. The air-raid wardens told us to get out of the house immediately and would not even give us time to get dressed. So with overcoats over our pyjamas we walked through the air raid to the Lyons Corner House in Coventry Street which at that time stayed open all night. We found it filled with people like ourselves, refugees from bombed or unsafe homes. Some of them slumped drowsily over their cups of tea, others talked and joked with a conspicuous gusto. But of complaints, self-pity, there was not even a suspicion. After listening to these voices for a while Hugh came out with a stream of questions and admissions which revealed more openly than ever before how deeply he felt at that time his involvement with England and her collective future (I hesitate to use the word greatness, for this is not a term Hugh would have used himself). This conversation came back vividly when I read his speech at the 1962 Brighton conference and heard other people's surprised comments on his 'thousand years of English history'.

This brief sketch of the ways Hugh Gaitskell travelled before he entered Parliament cannot do full justice to his whole itinerary. It has left out of account the various by-ways and deviations from his general progress. One of these by-ways must, however, be mentioned here, if only because at certain points it crossed and recrossed his political path. Throughout most of this period Hugh Gaitskell worked and regarded himself as a professional economist. His mathematical equipment was perhaps insufficient for him ever to have attained the very summit of the profession, but he was a very good

economist and promised to become an even better one. But
what struck me always in Hugh was not the excellence of his
economics but its whole-heartedness. He always set great store
by economics as an intellectual equipment and by economists
as solvers of economic problems. In Hugh's parlance 'the man
is an economist' was not merely a description but a commenda-
tion. Unfortunately, his growing involvement with political
work prevented him from progressing as far and as fast as he
would otherwise have done, and his membership of Parliament and his public office stopped his progress altogether.
Even then he entered Parliament excellently equipped as an
economist. To the end of his days he could understand and
handle an economic argument better than anyone else holding
high office in this country.

Where his interrupted progress showed itself most was in
his undimmed admiration for economics and economists,
which I suspect reflected his nostalgia for the profession he had
to abandon. I also suspect that had he continued his progress as
an economist he might also have developed a more sceptical
attitude to economic argumentation. I certainly do not know
of any truly outstanding economist with the requisite scholarly
knowledge of the subject—Samuelson, Hicks, Solow, Arrow,
Joan Robinson—who have not seen through the claims of
economic theory as a self-sufficient source of economic
wisdom. In the 'thirties Hugh Gaitskell, when challenged—
and challenged he frequently was—would be prepared to
admit that economics by itself could provide only a limited
contribution to the solution of problems, even where problems
happened to be mainly economic. Yet he never ceased to
approach economic problems as a theoretical economist. He
did so in the Ministry of Fuel and Power, in the devaluation
crisis of 1949, in the more recent discussions of England's
payment problems and again in his attitude to the Common
Market. And I have the impression that he listened to econom-

ists with far greater respect than to any experts in other fields of social and political enquiry. Whether this was a source of strength or a source of weakness to him in the 1950s and 1960s only those can say who observed him more closely in that period than I could.

I have not written the story of Hugh Gaitskell in the 'thirties and 'forties, but merely traced his emergence as a Gaitskellite. I have said very little of Hugh as a friend and a man, gay, affectionate, gentle and generous, yet as unyielding as a rock when it came to principles and loyalties. And I have said nothing at all of Hugh's non-political and non-intellectual pursuits —his acute literary tastes, his exalted view of D. H. Lawrence, his interest in modern painting, or his half-philistine attitudes to music and entertainments. I have left these sides of Hugh out, partly because I could think of one or two persons who could do this much better than I, but mainly because I do not believe this side of Hugh would have made a consecutive story. For it is surprising how little he changed as a man or as friend through the years in which I knew him. I met him for the last time a week or two before his final illness at an intimate dinner party at the Kaldors after a meeting of socialist economists in Cambridge, who had gathered to demonstrate to Hugh their support for his stand on the Common Market. He was obviously pleased to find himself on the same side as the economists whose economics he greatly admired, and yet amused that he should now have become a hero to some of the people to whom, in his own words, he had been 'a fascist beast' only a few weeks previously. But to me (we had a few days previously exchanged letters about the Common Market in which we recorded the parting of our ways) it was a nostalgic and a reassuring experience to watch and to hear him speak and react as he might have done at the University College dinner thirty-five years ago.

HOW HE CAME TO LEEDS

Marjorie Brett

It was in October 1936 that I first heard the name of Hugh
Gaitskell. Harry Charleton, the Labour Member of Parliament
for South Leeds, had let it be known that he would not be
fighting the next election, because as a member of the National
Union of Railwaymen he had reached the retiring age. My
father, who was the election agent for South Leeds, was
determined that the constituency should have a first-class
candidate, and with characteristic thoroughness and energy he
set out to find one. Although the Labour candidate for South
Leeds since 1924 had been a trade unionist who had contributed
generously to party funds, my father was too good a socialist
to let financial considerations influence him in his search.

His method was to find likely people and invite them to
South Leeds to speak at the wonderful open-air forum we had
in Cross Flatts Park which was in the constituency. As long as
I can remember, meetings had been held here on Sunday
mornings and they were so lively and controversial that they
went on long after one o'clock, so that many a South Leeds
voter arrived home to find an angry wife and a cold Sunday
dinner. In the autumn of 1936, G. R. Mitchison was one of the
speakers in Cross Flatts Park, and he learnt that we were looking for a candidate. This resulted in a letter from John Parker,

Member of Parliament for Romford and secretary of the New Fabian Research Bureau. My sister and I had become friendly with John Parker through the University Labour Federation and my father had met him when he came to speak in Leeds. Here is the letter:

Dear Mr. Brett,

Mr. G. R. Mitchison tells me that you are looking around for a candidate for the next election in South Leeds as Mr. Charleton is retiring and that you would welcome the suggestion of some good names. I am therefore taking the liberty of sending you some names of people of various views and talents all of whom would be very useful to the Party in the House of Commons which so greatly needs strengthening in personnel.

a. Hugh Gaitskell, a lecturer at University College, London. A first-rate speaker; the runner-up in the recent selection conference for Clay Cross. He fought Chatham in the last election. An authority on finance, foreign and colonial questions.

b. E. F. M. Durbin, a lecturer at the London School of Economics. An economist and authority on credit questions and planning. He fought Gillingham in the last election.

c. T. Reid, an authority on colonial questions. Did very well in Northwich in last election where he won over a large part of the Liberal vote.

d. Lady Noel Buxton, formerly M.P. for North Norfolk. General interest in women's questions and insurance. Was very good in House during the short time she was in.

e. Dr. Edith Summerskill who is a good speaker and a live and active woman. If there are many Catholics in the division, however, I should not recommend her as she is a strong advocate of birth control.

I hope you don't mind my writing to you in this way but hearing of your need I thought you would welcome suggestions and we really are in need of more good people in the House who can stand up to the Tories and not have an inferiority complex as many of our people unfortunately have.

Yours,
John Parker

My father and I went through this list together. Dr. Summerskill was definitely out because there was quite a large number
of Roman Catholics in the division and my father also felt
that a woman could not win South Leeds at that time. He
decided to find out more about Hugh Gaitskell and took the
opportunity of asking Hugh Dalton's opinion when he came
to speak in Leeds a month or two later. What he learnt impressed him sufficiently for him to try to arrange to meet Mr.
Gaitskell when he was next in London in April 1937, but
without success. Instead he received the following:

> I am very sorry to have missed you when you were in London last
> week. Mr. Parker will probably have told you that I was away
> on my honeymoon. I understand from him that you will be
> coming up again on 22nd May. If you have time I should be very
> glad to have a talk with you.

The meeting took place and, following it, Hugh Gaitskell
was invited to visit Leeds for the first time in August 1937,
when he spoke in Cross Flatts Park in the morning and at
another open-air meeting in another part of the constituency
in the evening.

In the meantime, however, my father had been making
enquiries about other possible candidates, particularly from the
National Union of Railwaymen. Two of their members, Dai
Jones and W. T. Proctor, were also invited to visit South
Leeds, and during August they also spoke in Cross Flatts Park.
My father gave firm orders to members of the executive
committee of the South Leeds Divisional Labour Party to
attend the meetings in the park whenever one of the possible
candidates was speaking, and he also arranged for one of the
youngest members, Mr. William Goodwill, now Chairman of
the South Leeds Labour Party, to move that Hugh Gaitskell
be put on the short-list. My father and other members of the
party thought that they would be able to choose for the short-
list the member of the NUR they wished. They were surprised

and annoyed to find that the Leeds members of the NUR had the right to make the nomination and that no other NUR member would be able to be included in the short list. The railwayman chosen was W. T. Proctor, and the feeling that he had been forced on South Leeds put him at a disadvantage, especially with the non-trade union section of the executive committee. My father had been strongly in favour of Hugh Gaitskell from his first meeting with him, but he knew that a trade unionist who had financial backing would stand a very good chance of being chosen.

There were finally three names on the short list, Hugh Gaitskell, W. T. Proctor and Evelyn Walkden, another trade unionist. Unfortunately, the first selection conference was abortive. It was held in September 1937 and my father only invited to it the men and women whose names had been sent in as delegates at the Annual General Meeting at the beginning of the year. Other affiliated organizations which had not bothered to nominate delegates in January, claimed the right to do so for the selection conference, and they were upheld in their view by Labour Party officials from Transport House. Another conference, therefore, had to be held a few weeks later in November. Before then Mr. Walkden withdrew because he felt that if a trade unionist was to have the seat, it should be another railwayman. This left Hugh Gaitskell and Mr. Proctor in the short list. The odds were against Gaitskell because the meeting was packed with trade union delegates; also he could offer no financial assistance. Yet by a few votes he was chosen.

From his first meeting with him, my father had decided that Hugh Gaitskell was the right man for South Leeds even though his nomination would mean that the constituency could no longer afford a full-time agent. Not until after he had been selected did the new candidate announce that he would pay something towards the party funds. This enabled my father to continue as a part-time agent and he acted as such until after the General Election of 1945.

Until the beginning of the war, Hugh Gaitskell paid many visits to South Leeds. He spoke frequently in Cross Flatts Park and at other meetings in the division. He attended social evenings, whist drives, fête days and summer outings to Scarborough and the Lake District. He tried to meet personally in the homes of the leading party members all the active people in South Leeds Labour Party and he paid the first of his many visits to the working-men's clubs where he met men who were not active in politics and learnt what they thought about current problems. He was often accompanied by his wife and she also became well known to the people in the division and particularly to the members of the women's sections of the Labour Party. He also wrote frequently for the *Leeds Weekly Citizen* and a monthly article for the *South Leeds Worker*, a small Labour paper which was distributed free to constituents.

We in South Leeds never understood the charge that Hugh Gaitskell found it difficult to mix with ordinary people. By his easy friendliness, his charm of manner and his complete unconsciousness of class-distinction, he gained the liking and admiration of all those in South Leeds who came in contact with him. He cared about people and was always ready to praise and thank those who helped him, or to visit or write to those who were ill or in trouble. My mother, who was one of his greatest admirers, used to say that she had never heard him say an unkind word about anyone. He and she found a common interest in gardening and in April 1939 there was an interesting reference to this activity in one of his letters:

> It has been beautiful weather here the last few days. I have done a lot of gardening and alternate that with writing a book on 'Money'. But the situation is disturbing! Whenever I hear the news I drop the book and get on with the digging. It seems a good deal more important.

There were two occasions after this when we nearly lost Hugh Gaitskell as candidate for South Leeds. The first time was on the outbreak of war in September 1939. A letter dated 8 September, 1939, says:

> I am not writing officially yet and would prefer you not to put anything absolutely definite before the EC for the simple reason that I don't know what I can put before them. I think it would be best if you simply told them (*a*) that I had been appointed to a post in the Ministry of Economic Warfare (*b*) that my salary is not much more than half my present earnings (*c*) that I do not see how I can do much as a candidate—I should have no time and as a Civil Servant *pro tem* I could not very well make speeches —(*d*) that I do not see how I can go on paying £100 a year to the division (*e*) that I will in any case continue till the end of this year (*f*) that I do *not* want to sever all connection with South Leeds. It's of course possible that I may get promoted some time in which case I could probably pay something tho' one must not forget heavier taxation. On the other hand if I am drafted into the army I should have even less and it would be then virtually impossible. On the whole I would prefer it if you simply told them the position and found out the general reactions. I don't think any decision should be taken until the situation is clearer. I also propose to consult one or two people this end as there must be many others who are in the same position as both of us.

From the next letter dated 14 October, 1939, it appears that the South Leeds executive committee expressed a wish to keep him as candidate whatever the circumstances:

> Many thanks for your letter with its news about the EC meeting. I naturally very much appreciate the resolution. It is very decent of them. Since I last wrote I have seen Dalton and discussed matters with him. He was very against my withdrawing from the constituency which indeed I did not want to do unless compelled and did not see why my present job should involve any such withdrawal. Indeed there is no more reason why I should than any candidate or MP who is on active service. Dalton also said that while I could not very well address public meetings,

I might come up and see as many as possible of our people some time. So if and when I get a holiday I will try and arrange it.

A letter the following month informed my father that the university would make up his salary to what it was before the war broke out so he would continue to pay his contribution to party funds. He hoped the executive would keep my father on as part-time agent: 'As I am sure the EC will agree, it is extremely important that Party activities and organization should be maintained despite the war.'

During the next few years Hugh Gaitskell made occasional visits to South Leeds to attend social evenings and party meetings, and to meet leading members of the party. He obviously regarded this as very important, because many of his letters contain sentences such as this: 'I will, as you suggest, come up for the March social. What I should like then would be a talk with the leading people in the party—private—to discuss future organizational problems rather than matters of policy.' Travelling was not easy in those days—he once spent eight hours getting from Leeds to London and had to stand in the corridor all the way.

During 1944 and early 1945 a good many of his letters to my father deal with the question of speakers for meetings and it is obvious that they were preparing for a General Election. Meetings were arranged at which Ivor Thomas, Glenvil Hall and Creech Jones were to speak, and Hugh himself said he would try to come to Leeds more frequently in 1945. Yet as the prospect of a General Election came nearer, we were shocked to hear that he was ill and might not be able to fight the election. The first news of his illness came in a letter dated 24 March 1945, in which he said that he was to see a heart specialist on 4 April. The next, written a few days later, is in his wife's handwriting. The specialist had prescribed three weeks in bed with complete rest, followed by two months' convalescence. Mrs. Gaitskell described the trouble as a minor case of coronary thrombosis, but because it came as the result of five years' overwork and strain, it meant that complete rest was the only possible treatment. Naturally, his main concern at this time was the election, which it was felt would come any time in the next six months. He wrote:

> I asked the specialist about the election and my own doctor who was there, and I think you ought to know that they were both discouraging, though not to the extent of positively forbidding me . . . they thought the date of the election made a good deal of difference . . . you can well imagine my feelings on the whole matter. To give up now would be a bitter blow and not only to me but to you as well who have helped me so much. For this reason I am prepared to take some risk but obviously one cannot go too far. I realize, of course, that I cannot wait long and that if I have to drop out, the party must be given time to find someone to take my place.

I can well remember my father's reaction to this. He was determined to have Hugh Gaitskell as the candidate for South Leeds and he was ready, if necessary, to fight the election without the candidate being there. He knew also that he could carry the members of the party with him, for Hugh was by this time very popular indeed with all the active members of the party. In April 1945, there seemed to be no urgency about the matter. Mrs. Gaitskell wrote at this time:

> As regards the election, we of course agree that there is no need to take any further action for the present. Fortunately it looks more and more as though it will not come until October. If so, Hugh feels that he ought to be fit enough to go through with it. He has to see the specialist again at the beginning of July which is also the end of his convalescence period.

Then in May came the news that the election was to take place on 5 July and, at the request of Hugh Dalton, Lord Horder was asked to examine Mr. Gaitskell and give a final opinion as to whether he should be allowed to fight the election. Dalton sent a copy of the letter which he had received from Lord Horder to my father. Lord Horder said:

Mr. Gaitskell is, as you know, convalescing from a heart illness. Given some limitation of effort over the next three months there is no reason why he should not be able to continue his political activities without prejudice to his health.

With regard to the coming election, however, Dr. Gosset and I are both of the opinion that Mr. Gaitskell should only consent to be a candidate for the South Leeds constituency on terms. These are:

1. That he should not arrive in the constituency earlier than a fortnight before the election day.
2. That his public appearances should be limited to two in any one day, only one of which should be a 'set' public meeting indoors.

If the local committee consents to accept Mr. Gaitskell as their candidate upon these conditions I feel sure I can rely upon it to see that they are carried out loyally.

The local committee did consent to these terms and my father, with the help of Hugh Dalton, set about acquiring a team of first-class speakers to come to the help of South Leeds. Attlee promised to speak at the nomination meeting, and other speakers included Arthur Greenwood and Dalton himself. The latter wrote: 'I have been thinking much of South Leeds and its standard bearer during these last weeks. May he carry the flag to victory! I will do all I can to help you and him to win.'

Two days after Lord Horder's letter, Hugh Gaitskell wrote to my father a very long letter with suggestions about meetings, photographs, the election manifesto and other election affairs. He concluded: 'We've defeated the doctors, now we can smash the Tories.'

This he proceeded to do, though it was obvious that he was a very sick man during the election campaign. My father, too, had suffered a coronary thrombosis during the war years and had lost his old energy and vigour, so with both the agent and candidate unable to give of their best, things might have gone badly. Yet by nine o'clock on the night of the election, we knew we had won—although the result was not to be announced until three weeks later because of the servicemen's votes—and a crowd of workers cheered him outside the main committee room before he left to go back to London. One local worker put Hugh Gaitskell's majority at 8,000 or so, but Hugh himself thought it might be 5,000, 'which is quite good enough for me'. In the event it was 10,402.

This was the last time my father was to act as election agent and before the result was announced, Hugh wrote thus to my father:

> In dour Yorkshire, people are not in the habit of paying compli-
> ments—as you have so often told me. But you are still for the
> most part Irish and I have been born and bred in the warmer
> South, so we may be permitted some extravagance in the matter.
>   I do want you to know how very grateful I am to you for
> everything you have done for me and with me ever since the far
> off days of 1937. Good advice, kindness, sympathy, encourage-
> ment—all have been showered upon me. And at the end, I know
> quite well it was *you* who were taking the really serious risks.
> I only hope that you never have cause to regret it. I realise you
> must now leave this particular ship to make its own way—
> having so to speak piloted it down the river to the open sea.

CIVIL SERVANT AND MINISTER

Douglas Jay

It was in the Labour Party, not at school or at Oxford, that I met Hugh Gaitskell. He left Winchester in 1924, two years before I did; and I overlapped with him one year only at New College, 1926–7. Though I knew him by sight, since he was pointed out at school as the man who would win the junior cross-country race (which he did not), I am not sure that we ever spoke to one another. Both of us supported the Labour Party whole-heartedly from 1926; but he was quickly plunged at Oxford into a world of economics and politics, while I stuck to philosophy (on which Hugh was never at his strongest) and history, until the storm of the Great Depression burst in 1929–33, and the strange spectacle of a hungry world growing hungrier, and less and less able to use its existing productive capacity, unfolded itself before us all.

Here was not only an inhuman tragedy, but a genuine intellectual puzzle. Pretended solutions of it rained thick and fast from the printing presses, in and out of the universities, and all those with active minds chased them remorselessly. It was in this chase in the autumn of 1933 that I was immensely struck by Hugh Gaitskell's contribution to G. D. H. Cole's symposium *What Everybody wants to know about Money*, in which he analysed Major C. H. Douglas's then famous theory that the depression was due to an inevitable failure of the credit machine. He showed with extraordinary lucidity, and the combination of honesty and clarity which became so celebrated later on (and fascinated me then), that there was indeed a failure of the monetary machine, but not of the kind Major Douglas believed. The implication of this was that the established economic system was not merely unjust—as all could see—but inefficient, wasteful and out-of-date. Here it seemed to me was the agenda for our generation; and here in this young man at least one of the minds most likely to attack it.

So we arranged to lunch. This was either at the end of 1933 or early in 1934. Hugh was working at University College, London, as an economics tutor. I went to Gower Street, and met him in a passage of that ugly building. He was wearing a light sort of holiday suit, and looked to me more like a student than a don. One had the sense, for once right, that this was a curtain-raiser, and that we should probably meet again. As it turned out, I knew him closely from this moment for nearly thirty years; worked with him for most of them; discussed almost every issue with him; seldom if ever disagreed; was hardly ever separated for more than a week or two; and formed for both his abilities and character a respect which gradually deepened into admiration.

It was unhappily necessary in the mid-1930s to fight the intellectual and political battle for social democracy on two fronts. First was the main front against reaction, stupidity and deflation, represented in its contemporary Anglo-Saxon form by the old economics and the City of London (popularly associated with Mr. Montagu Norman); and at its Teutonic worst by Hitlerism. But the issue was also clouded by the dogmatic Marxists who muddled the intellectual arguments, compromised on the central issue of free government, and so confused the political effort. Hugh Gaitskell never wobbled on either of these fronts. He did not think it necessary to be an ephemeral Marxist at the University (as though genu-flecting for safety to some heathen deity) and only to recover one's balance afterwards. So his group of closest friends and colleagues naturally tended to be those who believed equally in drastic redistribution of wealth, the British tradition of Parliamentary Government without qualification, and the building up of an international rule of law enforced through some world authority and if necessary defensive alliances. Hugh never suffered from the illusion of supposing that good causes would prevail automatically without having to be fought for.

These sympathies naturally brought him and the rest of us closest in spirit to Hugh Dalton, Clem Attlee and Herbert Morrison among the leaders of the Labour Party. Of the younger generation, Evan Durbin was—as he always remained —Hugh's most constant companion and colleague, and co-operator in almost every joint enterprise. Durbin's death in Cornwall in 1948, when rescuing his daughter and another girl from drowning, was one of the worst blows Hugh ever sustained: and he felt it very keenly indeed. Others associated with these two before the war were Robert Fraser (then leader-writer on the *Daily Herald*, now of the ITA), Francis Williams, John Wilmot and Maurice Webb (later Minister of Food). Frank Pakenham, always a very close personal friend, was also converted to the Labour Party in the mid-1930s. These and others of us concentrated on two main centres of discussion: the New Fabian Research Bureau, founded by G. D. H. Cole, which held crowded week-end conferences and livened up the old Fabian Society, and the more informal lunch or dining club known as the XYZ.

The main credit for founding and steering the latter must go to Sir Vaughan Berry, then assistant manager of the Union Discount Company and a lifelong supporter of the Labour Party. The feeling was shared in 1931 between him and a number of his City and City journalist friends, and Hugh Dalton, as well as by us among the under-thirties, that the party should never again allow itself to be so steeped in economic amateurism, and outmanœuvred by the professionals, as it had been in August 1931. So this group met, purely informally and privately, usually in the evening in members' flats, to try to sort things out, and (at first) to advise Hugh Dalton. Its other members included at times (besides Berry, Evan Durbin and Hugh Gaitskell), Francis Williams, George Strauss, J. H. Lawrie, Bill (now Lord) Piercy and others from the banking world. Most of us in 1934–5 expected this group to last a few months. In fact, with slight wartime interruptions, and evolving membership, it has continued to meet regularly ever since.

We first set ourselves to analyse in advance how a Labour Government should meet the foreign exchange and balance of payments problems that might complicate the carrying out of official Labour policy. But as the 1930s wore on, Hugh Gaitskell's conviction was generally accepted by the rest of us that war against Hitler was almost inevitable; and we decided to discuss systematically throughout 1938–9 the practical problems of running an all-out war economy—with the help of some who had experience of 1914–18. Of those concerned, Hugh Gaitskell, Evan Durbin, Vaughan Berry and several others in fact later became war-time Civil Servants organizing the industrial war effort.

In all this Hugh never behaved as a leader—not even as *primus inter pares*—but always as a sensible, above all candid, and valued member of the group. Yet it was at one of these round-the-room arguments—perhaps in 1936—that I vividly remember for the first time remarking to myself that he possessed a particularly penetrating common sense. Others were clever; but he gave one the right answers. His rather undistinguished workaday language, one realized, was always intended to convey facts and not conceal them. This was in

George Wansbrough's flat in Bloomsbury; an irrelevant point which I clearly recall because of the still more irrelevant accident that Wansbrough happened to keep parrots and other creatures in a cage in his flat. I was watching the antics of this part of the audience—such are the oddities of real life—at the moment when Hugh made the contribution which printed this impression indelibly on my mind.

But there was one other quality which already in the early 1930s distinguished him from many contemporaries of similar upbringing. He never shrank from all the tedious and exhausting routine of professional politics, which at the time drove so many fastidious, if weaker, spirits into more cloistered professions. (We had been adequately warned, it seemed to me, by the liberal German professors who thought politics unclean, and were quietly removed in the night by Hitler's Brownshirts.) In the General Election of 1935, fought on the issue of Abyssinian aggression and collective security, which fully aroused Hugh's strongest convictions, he and Evan Durbin were already standing as official Labour candidates in neighbouring Chatham and Gillingham respectively. I admired their early proficiency in street corner oratory, in the intervals of addressing envelopes and folding 'literature' on their behalf. Much as Hugh cared for academic values and dispassionate economics, I suspect that serious politics—with Hitler looming over us—was already more real to him. He had embarked at University College on research into the theory of capital, with the idea of publishing something later; but the war intervened. He gave, however, a great deal of time and scrupulous trouble to advising on my own book, *The Socialist Case*, on which I rashly embarked, with far less qualification than he, after the 1935 Election, in order to expound popularly our joint social-democratic non-Marxist views.

Yet Hugh's greatest qualities were of the kind, because they disdained show, which are not revealed quickly—and to unperceptive eyes hardly at all. It was not so much these social, academic or electioneering activities which in themselves disclosed his rare depth and strength of character. It was rather his ever-growing and hardening conviction throughout the 1930s—overriding by the time of Munich—that not only was Hitlerism a deadly menace to everything of value in modern civilization, but that Hitler meant war and could only be stopped by force or the threat of force. Hugh's greatest strength was his honesty in refusing to pretend that any sort of weakness or pacifism, anything indeed short of collective resistance by all possible means and all possible countries, could avert the danger. It was only in denunciation of appeasement that I saw him become passionate in those years. All this naturally brought him into close harmony with Hugh Dalton, and into collision with the pacifists and illusionists who—simultaneously or alternatively—wanted to resist Hitler and weaken the British armed forces. Hugh Gaitskell's view on this overriding issue was so strong and uncompromising that by the time of Munich itself he was forced into disagreement with some of his nearest friends (Robert Fraser and, even to some extent, though there was no personal breach, Evan Durbin).

Full perception of Hugh's unique combination of strength of purpose and understanding, however, did not come to me until we were all forced to face up finally to this dilemma, and make our choice. About ten days after the Munich week-end, while Quintin Hogg was standing in the Oxford by-election as an enthusiastic supporter of Chamberlain's Munich policy and Lord Dunglass (later Lord Home) was faithfully following Neville Chamberlain to and from Munich, amid a general atmosphere of folly and blindness, Hugh Dalton invited about fifteen members of the non-pacifist wing of the Labour Party to his flat near Victoria; and asked each in turn what they thought should be the policy of the Labour Party in this country towards Hitler, now that

Chamberlain had caved in. Those present included (according to my memory, which may be fallible—I have no record) Leonard Woolf, Kingsley Martin, Philip Noel-Baker, Evan Durbin, Robert Fraser, John Wilmot, Hugh Gaitskell and some other foreign policy experts, whom I cannot recall, besides myself. (Robert Fraser and Leonard Woolf confirm my memory of this meeting, and Leonard Woolf informs me that it was on 19 October, 1938.) This was at the moment of deepest gloom. Hugh Gaitskell spoke, however, in the strongest and most unyielding terms, as did Dalton, in favour of 'resistance' to Hitler by all practicable means, including military force. Only a small minority (including Noel-Baker) of those present supported him unreservedly. This experience filled me, I admit, with the blackest despondency. If this (I said to Hugh on the way home in the Underground) is the state of mind of the saner half of the Labour Party, how can they stiffen a rotten Chamberlain? And how can a thus wobbly Britain stiffen a rotten France? And what, seriously, can then stop Hitler long enough to give Roosevelt time to come to the rescue? He replied, with the utmost confidence, that a few of us would stiffen the Labour Party; that the Labour Party and Churchill would stiffen the country; that this country would stiffen France; and that we should then survive until Roosevelt joined in one day. At this moment we reached Charing Cross, and changed on to different Tubes.

From one obscure individual to another in the Underground, this did not seem perhaps a very powerful argument. But it was spoken with such force, clarity and conviction that I was not merely reconvinced of the impossibility of acting on any other assumption; but travelled home astonished that I could have known someone apparently so well for five years without recognizing his extraordinary reserve of underlying strength— 'Will like a dividing spear', as John Strachey aptly quoted from Matthew Arnold after Hugh's death. To me it illuminated,

once for all, what the next twenty-five years gradually unfolded to a larger audience. The tenacity of his stand against
Stalinism in 1948–51, and his massacre of the arguments for a
juvenile neo-pacifism in 1959–60, were only the fruits of a long
and consistently held conviction wrung out of bitter experience
in these earlier years.

Meanwhile, in that dreadful winter of self-deception,
1938–9, he worked day in and day out to convert the doubters,
and above all to persuade faint hearts in the Labour Party that
wars could not be fought without arms. By the time of the
invasion of Prague in March 1939, no doubts could remain
(except among Chamberlain's little clique, where the blind still
misled the blind); and Hugh was joyfully reunited with his
natural friends and colleagues—who freely now admitted that
he had been right. It was after Munich, because of his stand at
Munich, that he was first recognized as a leader among his
friends. Immediately after the seizure of Prague, he proposed
the bold venture of trying to persuade the official leaders of the
Labour Party to support conscription, if the Chamberlain
Government would support 'Conscription of Wealth' in
return; so that we could get a united national effort. It happened
that I had been advocating an annual capital tax on personal fortunes (what has now been revived under the popular name of a
'wealth tax') as a means of raising revenue needed for defence.
Hugh arranged that he, Evan Durbin and I should visit Attlee as
Leader of the Opposition at the House just before the Budget
of April 1939, and suggest that the Labour Party should put
forward this tax as its war-time version of 'conscription of
wealth' and offer to accept military conscription in return. To
our surprise—being just two Parliamentary candidates and one
other rank-and-file member of the party—we were received in
the Leader of the Opposition's room by Attlee, Dalton (who
was wholly with us), Morrison, Alexander and Shinwell.
Hugh argued his case so forcibly that those present were

favourably enough impressed by the plan to present it to the
Parliamentary Party. Here, however, the traditionalists still
narrowly prevailed; and the party committed the extraordinary folly—which above all we hoped to avert—of failing to
support conscription in April 1939. Understandably perhaps,
some still argued that the war could be fought if necessary
without this extreme; but we had done our best.

From Munich onwards, Hugh had never doubted that war
must come, and that the organization of the British war effort
for a long struggle would be the initial task. He moved,
therefore, through the official recruiting machinery to the
Ministry of Economic Warfare in September 1939, and started
work in its Intelligence Department as a temporary Principal.
David Eccles and Edwin Plowden were among his colleagues.
A scrupulous regard for official secrets (for which those
of us who worked as temporary Civil Servants felt all the
zeal of converts) prevented us from discussing Departmental business with those in other Ministries, or indeed with
most in our own; so I never heard nor enquired about the
details of Hugh's work in the first eight months of the phoney
war. All that one knew was that he found himself intensely
interested in the working of the Government machine and the
whole problem of efficiency in large-scale organizations. It was
an adventure to him, as indeed to many others, rather than a
tedious routine; and above all a vast relief to be fighting Hitler
with all one's working energy, rather than just verbally as in
the previous six stifling years. The Ministry of Economic
Warfare was of course concerned with 'pre-emption', the
Naval blockade of Germany and the 'Navicert' system; but
hope soon faded that any effective pressure could be brought
to bear on Hitler by the methods of the phoney war.

It was therefore an exhilarating piece of good fortune for
Hugh when, the formation of the Churchill Government in
May 1940, and entry of Labour Ministers into it, brought

Hugh Dalton—his closest friend among senior politicians and strongest advocate of Hugh Gaitskell's own uncompromising anti-Nazi views—into the MEW as Minister. Dalton's motto was 'belligerency' at all times, on the model of Clemenceau's *Je fais la Guerre* in the first war. He at once made Gaitskell his Private Secretary, and so began an extremely close partnership, which continued—with only short breaks—up to 1951. To Gaitskell, after holding a fairly junior post in the Intelligence Department, the position of Secretary to the Minister, with its bird's-eye view of the whole Ministry, was novel enough to reconcile him for a time to the secretarial chores of fixing appointments, chasing files and so forth. It was always an advantage for a private secretary or personal assistant to know Dalton well. One of the latter's minor failings was a tendency to shout aggressively at his officials when he was impatient or suspicious. Those who knew him realized that, if he was being unreasonable, one should shout back equally unreasonably; whereupon he would pipe down, usually with the greatest good humour. Hugh Gaitskell well understood this, and it was easier anyway for a temporary Civil Servant to treat Ministers in this way. Dalton also livened up the MEW by bringing in other young and active spirits including Gladwyn Jebb and Christopher Mayhew; and by all accounts at the time it was a vigorous and reasonably harmonious enterprise.

But as the blitz came and went, and Hitler invaded Russia, it became even clearer that the Naval blockade alone could not achieve much, and that it was the major service and munition departments which must win or lose the war. By the latter months of 1941 Hugh Gaitskell was very naturally becoming unwilling to be retained much longer as a mere Private Secretary and Principal. He consulted me, as I had been working in the Ministry of Supply for a year or so, about the possibility of joining us as the main expanding munition department.

Since a new post as assistant secretary was being created in the manpower section, I suggested Hugh as a candidate for this, with his approval. The hierarchy, however, took the view that they had not enough evidence of the aptitudes of this little-known temporary ex-don; and the job went to a thoroughly worthy character from my own section whose abilities I knew to be commonplace compared with Hugh's.

Once again, however, events threw Hugh Gaitskell forward and solved his problem. In February 1942, after the disasters of Pearl Harbour and Malaya, the Government was reshuffled, and Dalton became President of the Board of Trade, replacing Andrew Duncan, who to the great relief of the Ministry of Supply returned there as Minister in succession to Lord Beaverbrook. Dalton transferred Gaitskell to the Board of Trade as his Personal Assistant outside the official hierarchy, and made him an assistant secretary (rank in the Civil Service counts for a lot, even in war-time, because of its anonymity). This appointment partly rested on the somewhat jejune idea, common in the Labour Party before 1939, that a Labour Minister would do well to have by his side a political sympathizer who could supplement the official advisers. Gaitskell very soon found (as I did from similar hard experience with Dalton a year or two later and at No. 10 Downing Street in 1945–6) that such a being, unless he is exceedingly skilful, tends to find himself, in Churchill's phrase, 'brooding in ignorance on the work of others'. He needs an infinity of tact to stay where he is, and unrelenting persistence to move forward. During this period Hugh was mainly concerned with the highly controversial, and in the end abortive, plan to ration fuel. He also got to know the Board of Trade senior officials well, and learnt a great deal about Whitehall diplomacy. He was also more accessible to those of us outside his Department, if only at lunch-time or during fire-watching hours; and constantly pressed me to join the Board of Trade, which during 1942 and most of 1943 I did not feel able to do, since the Ministry of Supply remained far closer to the war effort.

Within a few months, however, Hugh had had enough of brooding, and was appointed to a full executive job as principal assistant secretary (a rank between assistant secretary and under secretary abolished after the war) in charge of price control, retail trade, and the film industry. This he appeared to find wholly absorbing and satisfying; and he disappeared as it were into a tunnel of steady, efficient, laborious administration. Working, myself, in the same Ministry in 1944 and 1945, I hardly seemed to meet him from one week to another. Indeed, it has always been a slight mystery to me why during these eighteen months, living near to him and working on the same floor of the same building, I seemed to see less of him than at any time in the previous ten years or next fifteen. One assumed at the time that it was because, as the end of the war and the planned industrial reconversion drew nearer, we were all so desperately busy with our own responsibilities in working hours, and with fire-watching and flying bombs out of them, as to leave no room for anything else.

The truth may have been, however, that Hugh had grossly overtired himself by his war-time exertions, and that this led to the mild heart trouble which appeared in the spring of 1945. This was the only period between 1933 and 1963 when he seemed basically tired. In the spring of 1945, as the German War ended and the Election approached, his malady was diagnosed as a slight heart attack. Hugh had of course been Labour candidate for South Leeds for nearly ten years; and now it suddenly seemed that, at the moment when the Election had at last come, he might not be able to stand. But on the advice of Lord Horder, he was allowed to do so with caution, and was duly elected with a large majority. By the autumn and to the vast relief of Hugh's friends, his heart was fully recovered, and never gave trouble again. When the

Labour Government was formed in July, however, he was judged to be not yet fit for full-time executive work; and for this reason was not, like Harold Wilson, immediately appointed a Junior Minister in the new Government.

Together with Evan Durbin, who had been elected MP for Edmonton, Hugh was thus left with a slightly easier life for six months, in which to pick up the oddities of Parliamentary procedure, get the hang of Parliamentary committees and make a maiden speech. In May 1946, Attlee made him Parliamentary Secretary to the Ministry of Fuel and Power, where Shinwell was Minister. This was a very happy choice. For, odd though it may have seemed to some, Hugh had always felt a very deep allegiance to the British miner. It was their cause in 1926 which brought him first into the Labour Party and into politics. It was with the Nottingham miners that he worked for the WEA after leaving Oxford. Sam Watson, leader of the Durham miners, was for long one of his closest friends. In his four difficult and crowded years at the Ministry of Fuel and Power, the bond was not forgotten on either side.

In 1946 the situation could hardly have been more difficult. It was clear to those who knew the facts within the Government machine that a serious fuel shortage was probable in the winter of 1946–7, unless exceptional measures similar to those adopted by the Ministry of Supply in the war (not including direction) were used to man up the coal industry throughout 1946. Those of us who had urged this for months past with only partial success were overjoyed to find Hugh Gaitskell's perceptive and receptive mind recruited to the Ministry of Fuel and Power, and we redoubled our efforts to get action in time. But there was still resistance to the idea of emergency measures, e.g. the maximum possible use of Polish ex-miners already in the country. Hugh laboured unremittingly through these rather agonizing months to avert the catastrophe; but he always took the view (some might not have done) that loyalty to one's Minister must be at least as important as campaigning for the right policy. This was one example of the exceedingly high place loyalty occupied in his scale of values.

When the long-feared crisis came in February 1947 (made finally inevitable by the persistent north-easterly gales) Hugh chanced to be in Yorkshire, and was at least able to apply emergency remedies by organizing lorry transport of South Yorkshire coal into beleaguered Lancashire. For some months after this the Government's main energies were devoted to planning and launching a long-term fuel and power development programme, hinging mainly on the huge expansion of electric power supplies, which has since in fact occurred. At last the problem was recognized as a programming and largely statistical one, not much assisted by oratory; and in October 1947 Hugh Gaitskell was made Minister of Fuel and Power, with Alf Robens as Parliamentary Secretary—another very fruitful partnership—and a clear remit from Attlee to cut out the chatter and stick to the figures.

This was the signal for a long period of steady achievement. For the first time Hugh Gaitskell was given a job which fully stretched his practical abilities. Only a month later, Dalton's resignation as Chancellor brought Stafford Cripps to the position of Chancellor and Minister for Economic Affairs with full co-ordinating authority over economic policy generally. For the first time, a Minister existed with clear and overriding responsibility for the balance of payments. Thus ended the well-meant but misconceived system of two parallel economic Ministers—Dalton as Chancellor and Herbert Morrison as a rather shadowy co-ordinator ('brooding in ignorance' much of the time through no fault of his own)—which had been copied from the war-time system. Unhappily, it was not fully realized till 1947 that the war-time system of a separate Treasury and Ministry of Production was effective just as long as there was no balance of payments problem, and the bill merely had to be sent to Washington; but far less workable when the balance of payments became the overriding issue. Failure to understand this was part cause of the 1947 convertibility crisis.

Hugh Gaitskell who had chafed at his impotence to avert this crisis in the summer months of 1947, was immensely relieved (despite deep personal regret over Dalton's resignation) at the concentration of economic responsibility in one Minister. Stafford Cripps' appointment of the planning staff under his authority, and of a rational structure of Cabinet Committees, brought the problem within grasp; and adapted the Whitehall machine to the needs of Marshall Aid and the OEEC. It also provided an admirable framework for Hugh's administrative talents. With surprising rapidity the United Kingdom economy responded to the change of policy and the prospect of Marshall Aid. Throughout 1948 production and exports rose rapidly, and a large balance of payments surplus reappeared in less than a year from the crisis of August 1947. It continued throughout 1948, 1949 and 1950.

In the years 1947–50 Hugh and his Department launched a major expansion programme in the electricity supply, gas and coal industries, overcame the fuel shortage, created a new oil refinery industry in this country—and incidentally carried through a gas nationalization Bill, involving a record Parliamentary marathon. Though less seen by the public, Hugh gave a major part of his time in these years to an extremely thorough review of the economic effects on the UK and Sterling Area of the world-wide operations of the British oil companies. The figures had never been worked out before; and nobody really knew whether Shell, BP and Burmah Oil were net dollar earners or spenders. When the results were tabulated, some Ministers thought that two or three noughts must have been added to them by mistake. It was realized that the earnings of these three companies were a major factor in the UK balance of payments and the strength of sterling, and that by a policy of 'substituting' sterling for dollar oil, and also by the building of refineries in the UK and sterling area, a further major easement of Britain's economic difficulties was achieved. (This and other references in this chapter to official deliberations are made purely from memory, and I have not consulted any official records.) Hugh Gaitskell was largely responsible for these exceedingly important reforms; and in the process BP and Shell became better acquainted with the needs and aims of the Government, as well as vice versa.

In this period, intimately as I had known Hugh for fifteen years, I found it hard to recognize in the accomplished and forceful Senior Minister either the argumentative economist of pre-war days or even the assiduous Civil Servant of 1943. Perhaps his most remarkable talent, viewed over his whole working-life, was his capacity—which I have known in nobody else—to emerge on a broader stage not merely as competent as on a smaller, but both *more* competent, and also more competent than his closest friends had in their heart of hearts expected. Sir Donald Ferguson, his Permanent Secretary at the Ministry of Fuel and Power, and a very experienced permanent Civil Servant who had been head of three Ministries and served even more Ministers of several parties, said to me with frankness one day after 1950 that Hugh Gaitskell was 'the most efficient Minister with whom I ever worked'.

In these years the Production Committee of the Cabinet, presided over by Stafford Cripps, did a great deal of practical business; and the Chairman did not suffer gladly, as was very well known, either loquacity, delay, obstinacy or indecision. One day the investment programme for the fuel and power industries, prepared by Cripps' planning staff (in consultation of course with the Ministry of Fuel and Power) was before the Committee. When his turn came, Hugh Gaitskell observed, with as much brevity as force, that he had not approved these figures; that nobody had the right to decide the Minister of

Fuel and Power's business; that he doubted the constitutional
rôle of the official Investment Programmes Committee; that
Ministers were responsible neither to the Cabinet nor to the
Prime Minister, but to Parliament; and that he was not going
to have his constitutional authority whittled away by one iota.
This was near mutiny. Senior Cabinet Ministers on the
Committee like Nye Bevan were visibly astonished at such
defiance of Stafford Cripps in the plenitude of his power by a
mere upstart Civil Servant turned Minister. But Cripps, to his
credit, looking grimly down his nose, thought otherwise. It
was his supreme and rare merit that he knew the difference
between a good argument and a bad one. The fuel and power
figures, he said amiably, would have to be reconsidered; and
he would ask the head of the Civil Service to advise on the
constitutional issue. Whether such advice was ever given, I do
not know; but nobody after this tried to push the Minister of
Fuel and Power around.

Hugh Gaitskell's critics might retort that this incident merely
illustrates his famous obstinacy and refusal to admit he was
wrong. It is certainly true that, when an issue seemed to him
to be clear, he was unwilling to pretend to be still in doubt.
But it is completely untrue that he would refuse to listen to
arguments, or think over a problem again, or examine new
facts or evidence if such really existed. At another meeting of
the Production Committee in these years, he had himself
proposed abandoning all open-cast coal working, in view of
the Coal Board's success in raising deep-mined output.
Boldly, perhaps, I questioned the wisdom of this, though less
informed on the details than he, and argued that so many
hazards surrounded the fuel situation as to make it advisable
to treat open-cast coal for a good many years yet as an insurance against contingencies. Hugh Gaitskell replied, contrary to
my expectations, that he would like to think about this a bit
longer. His paper was withdrawn, and open-cast production

continued for another ten years. This was not the reaction of a stupidly obstinate man.

But Hugh Gaitskell's reputation for exceptional qualities of character with senior Ministers, with most of his colleagues, and with the Civil Service was made in the dollar crisis of 1949. The Official Secrets Act forbids one to tell the full story, which would redound to Hugh's credit much more than anything yet publicly known; but this much can be said. The spectacular economic recovery of the UK in 1948 was checked after the spring of 1949, despite still rapidly rising production and exports, and a continued UK balance of payments surplus, by a sudden new-style American recession. Prices of primary commodities fell sharply; and the dollar earnings of the Sterling Area fell with them. The weekly dollar drain re-appeared for the first time since 1947. It had always been my view (and I think that of most economists) that the dollar-sterling exchange rate of $4.04, fixed on 3 September, 1939, could not possibly be held indefinitely after the war, when the relative economic weighting in the world of the United States and United Kingdom had dramatically tipped over. But of course there was no point in devaluing sterling into balance with the facts of the post-1945 world, until surplus capacity existed in UK exporting industries. To have acted earlier would simply have turned the terms of trade against us without increasing exports. By June and July of 1945, it became insistently apparent that, owing to the world recession started by the United States shake-out, such surplus exporting capacity existed. In the view of most of the experts, sterling must be devalued; and if so, effectively, to the true parity.

This, however, was an extremely serious step for Ministers to take. And unhappily, Stafford Cripps, worn down by persistent overwork into worsening ill-health, was forced to retire in July 1949, for two months' convalescence abroad just at the moment when economic opinion had become almost unanimous that devaluation to about $3.0 in September was the right, and indeed almost the only, remedy. In this situation, when every opportunity for delay and confusion existed, Hugh Gaitskell, who had been given part authority for Treasury policy under the PM in Cripps' absence, made up his mind clearly and decisively what needed to be done; convinced the doubters, including the Chancellor himself while abroad, and supervised all the arrangements (for which great credit should also be given to the official Treasury) with remarkable efficiency and absolute secrecy. In effect, at the moment of crisis, he took charge as the man who knew what needed to be done and was able to do it. It was this chapter which left no doubt in the minds of those few who knew the facts that, if Cripps' health failed, Hugh Gaitskell was the only possible Chancellor. His eventual appointment played such a part in provoking Nye Bevan's unfortunate resignation in 1951, with all its consequences, that the events of July–September 1949—unknown to most chroniclers of this period, because of the contemporary need for secrecy—were the really decisive factors in determining the subsequent leadership of the Labour Party and so much else.

In September 1949, Sir Stafford Cripps returned to the Treasury and Hugh Gaitskell to the Ministry of Fuel and Power. The excessively (in my view) deflationary 'consequential' measures of October and November 1949 were no direct responsibility of Hugh's. Nor did he favour Cripps' disastrous determination (opposed by all his colleagues) to hold the 1950 Election in February rather than May, which in its turn led to a Labour majority too small to continue in Parliamentary control longer than the autumn of 1951. After the February 1950 Election, however, and as a consequence of his decisive part in the events of 1949, Hugh was appointed Minister of State at the Treasury with a rank equal to that he previously held as Minister of Fuel and Power. Whether or not the Prime

Minister told him he would become Chancellor if Cripps were forced to retire, I do not know. It would be unlike Attlee to use one word where none would do. Hugh took over my previous work as Economic Secretary (I became Financial Secretary) and also a major share in preparing the 1950 Budget. It was exceedingly pleasant to be thus restored to close daily collaboration. Our first joint act was to persuade the Chancellor, with Nye Bevan's support, that the cut in the housing programme, made in the 1949 'consequential' measures from 200,000 a year (the maximum which softwood supplies then allowed) to 175,000, should be restored. Hugh Gaitskell showed himself even more eager for the change than Nye; and this—naturally not known to the public and never publicized by Hugh, despite all the later public controversy over charges for teeth and spectacles—should perhaps now be stated in fairness to him.

Hugh also devoted much time and effort during 1950 to the launching of the Colombo Plan, the strengthening of Commonwealth economic ties, and the negotiation of the highly successful European Payments Union. It was during a Commonwealth Finance Ministers' Conference at this time, over which he presided in Cripps' stead, that I recall feeling with fresh surprise that he was again, on a still larger stage, revealing powers which I had not realized he possessed. The Commonwealth Finance Ministers were at first, privately, a little disappointed to be received, not by the famous Sir Stafford Cripps, but by this much younger and to them largely unknown Minister. One could see their faces registering interest, then surprise and then appreciation, as he made his opening statement. By the end they were near unanimous in their praise. Was this the middle-grade amateur Civil Servant of five years before?

So, when Stafford Cripps was forced by ill-health to resign the Chancellorship outright in October 1950, there was no room for doubt, or, indeed, little change. Hugh Gaitskell became Chancellor—at a moment when everything looked set fair, but when in fact the worst storms since 1945 were about to break. It is sometimes now forgotten, in view of later years of stagnation, how much had been achieved by deliberate economic policy up to the end of 1950, and how successful Stafford Cripps' general strategy and planning had proved. Production, exports and investment had been rising rapidly and continuously for five years; the 1949 devaluation had corrected the post–1939 over-valuation of the £; the balance of payments had been in surplus for three years on end; and gold flowed in continuously (this is particularly often forgotten) from September 1949 to June 1951. Even the cost of living was surprisingly stable from September 1949 till after the outbreak of the Korean War in June 1950. For all these reasons it was possible to renounce further use of Marshall Aid in the autumn of 1950, over a year sooner than had been planned.

Had it not been for the Korean War (one can now see) the immediate post-1945 economic difficulties would have been overcome, and relaxation at home could have been combined —in an easier world context—with an assault on the long-term aims of faster growth in the British economy. Into this brightening picture burst the North Korean forces in the summer of 1950. For some months, however, the immensity of the economic consequences was not understood. It was realization of the probable length of the struggle which after a time induced the United States Government to embark on a huge strategic stockpiling policy. This forced up world prices of primary products at a headlong rate, and actually raised the price of United Kingdom imports by 40 per cent in twelve months. This would at any time have plunged the UK economy in crisis; and in the winter of 1950–1 it undid temporarily much of the advance achieved since 1947. The fundamental rise in production and exports of course remained. But the short-term

balance of payments and reserve position was again under-
mined; though it was remarkable that the gold reserve
even so stood at its post-war peak as late as June 1951. The
record of this year has been so perverted by propaganda that
the hard facts surprise even well-informed people. The simple
reality is this. In May and June the gold reserve was still rising;
and the Chancellor was mainly occupied in piloting an
extremely controversial Finance Bill through parliament with
a majority of six (which never fell below two). Before the end
of July measures were taken to restrict imports; and they would
have been followed by others in the autumn, had the Prime
Minister not decided that it was impossible to continue another
year without a bigger majority, and therefore asked for a
dissolution.

Hugh Gaitskell, however, was not merely faced with the
Korean economic unheaval, almost immediately on becoming
Chancellor. He was also faced by the menace of an aggressive
Stalin, who had launched the Berlin blockade only two years
before, and was now supporting—at least verbally—the
Chinese and North Korean armies in their war against United
Nations forces in Korea. Here undoubtedly the deep convictions which Hugh had formed in the Munich years played
a dominating part in his mind. He did not make the crude
mistake of confusing Stalin or Mao with Hitler. But he did
believe that military dictators were usually arbitrary and often
expansionist; and that military weakness among the democracies in this situation invited disaster. For this reason he
became convinced that, as in 1938–40, we must take some
deliberate economic risks to defend basic freedoms, and that
collective defence by the democracies offered far the best
chance of avoiding war this time. Some will think that time
has vindicated his judgement. At any rate, the firm policy
pursued has been more successful than the surrenders of 1935–8.
Peace has been preserved: and Stalinist truculence has been

supplanted by a far more conciliatory Soviet attitude and eventually by the Test Ban Treaty of 1963. This was after all the object of the exercise.

Hugh, therefore, holding these beliefs, was faced by a supremely difficult problem in the Budget of 1951. He had to finance the British contribution to a major strengthening of collective defence; he had to ward off the danger of a new balance of payments crisis; and he found a country weary of twelve years of sacrifice and high taxation. He resolved, none the less, to launch further major increases in social services; the first big rise of old-age pensions since 1946 was included in the 1951 Budget: and total social service expenditure was increased by £50 million. He believed, however, that if this were done, and taxes were raised at the same time, some restriction must be placed on the increase in spending on other services which were growing most quickly. It was this conviction, also strongly held, that led him into a review of the rapid rise in Health Service expenditure and so into unhappy conflict with Nye Bevan.

The Health Service had been exhaustively scrutinized during the preceding weeks by a Cabinet Committee consisting of the Ministers concerned, who did not include Nye Bevan, because he was Minister of Labour and no longer Minister of Health. In the end all major economies were abandoned; and a compromise reached on charges for artificial teeth and spectacles, costing only £13 million in 1951–2 and £25 million in a full year. This was really not a major issue. Indeed Bevan himself implicitly admitted that it was not, by inserting later in his resignation letter and speech a totally new argument about the defence programme being too large. Unfortunately, however, he learnt of the health proposals at just about the same time, before the 1951 spring Budget, as he heard that Herbert Morrison had been appointed Foreign Secretary. This news, coming on top of Hugh Gaitskell's appointment as Chancellor a few months earlier, unhappily if understandably provoked in Bevan a state of mind in which any change in his treasured Health Service appeared the last straw. It was one of those unfortunate issues where, in all reality, not much was at stake, but where it had become hard for either protagonist to retreat. Most of those concerned in the argument believed a compromise had been reached by which the charges were to be purely temporary, and limited to the period of the defence emergency. But Nye Bevan, it proved, was not satisfied with this after all.

It appeared to many of us that so small an element in the Budget (far smaller than the rise in other social spending) was not worth so much commotion. Indeed, I had one of my rare disagreements with Hugh Gaitskell and told him I believed that in the long run the saving would not prove worth the conflict caused, though I should have regarded it as excessive egotism, to push one's personal view on such an issue to the point of damaging one's colleagues. His answer (and that of others among his colleagues) was that you could hardly run a democratic Cabinet on the principle that, if there was a division of 18 to 2, the view of the 18 should prevail when X was one of the 18, but the view of the 2 should prevail when X was one of the 2. I found this a difficult argument to refute. For Hugh was a great believer in rational and straightforward methods of procedure.

Once again, therefore, he surprised everyone by his tenacity and firmness of purpose, and carried the day. The rest of the story is publicly known. Bevan, after many changes of mind, resigned, and a long and rather sterile controversy followed. Hugh Gaitskell's ruling motive throughout was his long-held determination, first, that the collective defensive strength of the democracies must be a crucial aim if peace was to be preserved; and secondly that joint decisions taken in Cabinet must be observed. Whether you agree with him or not, these are motives which all must respect; just as they must also respect Nye Bevan's anxiety to preserve what he sincerely regarded as a principle of social policy.

In the years after 1951 (with which this chapter is not mainly concerned) Hugh Gaitskell built up, on top of so much else, a remarkable Parliamentary reputation. His speeches denouncing the Suez policy were the finest made in the British House of Commons after 1945, excepting only Sir Stafford Cripps' speech on economic policy on 7 August, 1947, and not excepting many impressive post-war performances by Churchill and Bevan. A Parliamentary speech must be judged, in the last resort, by its power to convince opponents and change the course of official policy. This was achieved by Hugh's speeches on Suez, just as it was by the famous Norway debate of May 1940. The series of almost non-stop debates at the end of October and beginning of November 1956 made it impossible for Sir Anthony Eden (now Lord Avon) to continue his policy —one of the obvious facts almost totally overlooked by those who fall into the conventional fallacy of believing that Parliament has less influence over Prime Ministers and Governments today than a hundred years ago (when incidentally it hardly ever met in October or November at all). Suez proved the contrary.

One legend about Hugh Gaitskell's speeches at this time must be refuted here, since it is wholly false. This is the story that he changed his mind between August and November, and first acquiesced in the Eden policy, and afterwards attacked it. When he made his speech in the first debate on 2 August, he did not believe it possible that Eden should contemplate such a folly as the use of armed force on Egyptian soil. In spite of this, he included in this speech a warning passage about the absolute necessity of not transgressing the United Nations Charter by any rash action. As soon as he became convinced that Eden was really contemplating military action, he attacked such a policy with the gathering force which in the end compelled its abandonment.

Together with John Hynd, I saw Hugh immediately before the debate on 2 August to urge on him the necessity of declaring against any use of force or breach of UN principles. He replied that he knew from Eden's private assurances that nothing of this kind was intended. It did not then occur to him to question this, and he spoke (privately and publicly) under this impression. He agreed, however, on the advisability of inserting a warning about UN principles, but simply to provide against all contingencies however remote.

Immediately after this debate, I learnt from Fleet Street sources in daily touch with the Foreign Office that there were strong reasons for thinking that a military expedition was going to be prepared. When I informed Hugh Gaitskell of this at once before he left London for the August Bank Holiday week-end, he replied that he simply could not believe it, in the light of the assurances he had received from the Prime Minister. Not fully sharing Hugh's confidence this time, Denis Healey and I—in view of the reports reaching Fleet Street—wrote a letter to *The Times* which appeared on 7 August, and is on the record, formally stating the case against any use of military force on Egyptian soil. Hugh then returned to London, breaking his August holiday, and asked Eden for renewed assurances; and Eden's response again convinced him that nothing of the sort was contemplated.

Eden again in the September debate, for which Parliament was specially recalled, persuaded the House that no use of force was intended. It was not until after this that Hugh began seriously to suspect that a military expedition was being prepared; and then the tone of his speeches changed. Not unnaturally it changed even more sharply when Eden suddenly announced that the expedition had, in fact, been launched. Hugh remarked to me shortly after this that he would never believe anything said by Eden, in public or in private, again.

It is a little hard, in these circumstances, that Hugh should be blamed because his speeches in November were more critical than his speeches in August.

Even those who did not know Hugh Gaitskell closely were beginning to realize in 1959–62 that he was probably better fitted to be Prime Minister than any other party leader of this century. He had strength of character and courage denied to MacDonald or Baldwin; trustworthiness lacking in Lloyd George or Chamberlain; an understanding of the social and economic facts of the modern world denied to Winston Churchill; and an all-round intellectual equipment which Clem Attlee, despite all his other rare gifts, would not aspire to rival. To have claimed all this for Gaitskell would have seemed absurd to most people up till 1959–60; but not after. The timing of his death was thus as tragic as the loss to the nation was irreplaceable. Yet, despite all this, it is not mainly for any of these qualities that he is, and will be, remembered most thankfully by those who knew him best. Rather is it his deep and unchallengeable loyalty to the people as well as to the causes that earned it, which, when one looks back in admiration over thirty years, stand out as even more precious and more nearly unique.

WINNING THE TRADE UNIONS

1. Lord Williamson

The war ended on 8 May, 1945, and on 23 May Mr. Attlee, as he then was, tendered his resignation to the King. This was the end of the Coalition Government, and polling day to elect the new Parliament was on 5 July.

I had been for some time an Industrial Officer of my union, the National Union of General and Municipal Workers. By coincidence rather than design, however, I was adopted at the last minute for the Brigg Division of Lincolnshire. When the votes were eventually counted—there was a long delay owing to the need to bring home the Service vote—I found myself elected. Thus it was that when Parliament assembled I found myself sitting on the same Benches as Hugh Gaitskell who had been elected for South Leeds.

In the new Government, Hugh Dalton, whom I had known on the National Executive Committee of the Labour Party, was Chancellor of the Exchequer. He was anxious to keep in touch with Back Bench opinion on financial matters and with this in view invited a number of people to serve as a financial group. I was one of these and so was Hugh Gaitskell and this was my first meeting with him.

I only remained in the House of Commons until March 1948. Towards the end of 1946 I had been elected as General

Secretary of my union in succession to Mr. Charles Dukes and
the view was taken that to hold this office was incompatible
with membership of the House of Commons. But until I left
the House I was the senior trade union man on the Labour
Benches. During this period I had much to do with Hugh
Gaitskell.

In September 1951 he was invited, as Chancellor of the
Exchequer, to speak at the Trades Union Congress at Blackpool
and he greatly impressed the trade union leaders, particularly
on the question of wage restraint and incomes policy—the
speech deserves re-reading in the light of discussions on
economic planning today. The following June he spoke at the
Annual Conference of the National Union of General and
Municipal Workers, of which he was a member. This was
the first of many visits on which he made a considerable
impact on the delegates and showed both his authority and his
understanding of the trade union movement. I was not the
only one who grew to believe that he had a very important
rôle to play in the future of the Labour and trade union
movements.

The early years of the 1950s were, of course, marked by the
sharp disagreements within the Labour Party, associated with
Bevanism. The trade union movement, and particularly many
of the larger trade unions, believed that these were doing the
party much harm, and found themselves increasingly in support of the position which Hugh Gaitskell had taken up.

At the 1952 Labour Party conference the Bevanites made an
almost clean sweep of the Constituency section of the National
Executive Committee and in particular got rid of Hugh
Dalton and Herbert Morrison. Ironically, both had played an
important part in getting the Party Constitution revised in
1937 to give seven members in a separate section elected by the
constituency parties alone: both had served on the Committee
for many years with distinction. Following his defeat, Hugh

Dalton did not appear anxious to enter the arena again. Herbert Morrison on the other hand wished to return to the National Executive Committee. It was my view that his return would be very much in the interests of the party.

The Treasurer of the party at that time was Arthur Greenwood, but unfortunately his health had been failing and it was doubtful how long he could remain effective in his job. It was for this reason that a number of trade union leaders, including myself, put forward the name of Herbert Morrison to contest the treasurership with Arthur Greenwood at the 1953 Conference at Margate. At the same time a resolution was placed on the Agenda for an amendment to the constitution of the party whereby the Deputy Leader of the Parliamentary Party would become *ex-officio* a member of the National Executive Committee. As Herbert Morrison was the Deputy Leader, the combination of his nomination as Treasurer and of the proposed amendment to the constitution was a concerted effort to return him to the National Executive Committee. I came to have grave misgivings, however, about Herbert Morrison going forward in a contested election in view of Arthur Greenwood's health. I believed that Morrison would win, but thought it would be unfortunate in view of the long and distinguished service which Arthur Greenwood had given to the movement. My view that the contest ought not to take place was strengthened when on the eve of the Conference the National Executive Committee agreed to support the resolution which would result in the Deputy Leader of the Parliamentary Party becoming a member of the National Executive Committee.

Accordingly, I put it to Morrison that he ought to withdraw. He saw the point, but was not at all anxious to upset Arthur Deakin, the leader of the Transport and General Workers' Union, who had been pressing his claim strongly. I then asked Morrison, would he be prepared to withdraw if I myself spoke to Deakin and asked him whether he would object? Morrison agreed, and when I put the case to Deakin he said that there would be no ill-feeling if Morrison did not go forward.

Thus Morrison withdrew and Arthur Greenwood was elected unopposed. Nevertheless, the need to find a successor to Greenwood was very much in mind and shortly after the Margate Conference I put it to Arthur Deakin that we ought to be thinking of a successor. I then mentioned to him the name of Hugh Gaitskell, and Deakin agreed that he was someone whom he could support. Clearly, the backing of both the Transport and General Workers' Union and my own union was likely to be crucial in any contest.

Arthur Greenwood died in June 1954. Meanwhile, in April, Aneurin Bevan had resigned from the Shadow Cabinet on a disagreement about Labour's attitude towards the South-East Asia Treaty Organization. It was clear that when the time came Gaitskell would not be allowed to become Treasurer unopposed. In the event, however, the vote at the Labour Party conference in October 1954 was 4,338,000 votes for Hugh Gaitskell and 2,32,000 votes for Aneurin Bevan.

This was a decisive turning-point for Hugh Gaitskell. Previously, as he was not a member of the National Executive Committee, he had been obliged at conference to speak only from the floor. To many delegates he was a comparatively unknown figure, despite his period as Chancellor. Now, as a member of the National Executive Committee, he became as important in the movement as a whole as he was already in the Parliamentary Party.

The evidence of this came in his first major speech from the platform at the party conference at Margate in 1955. He spoke in reply on the Wednesday afternoon of conference week to a debate on nationalized industries. He already had behind him the knowledge that in a second contest for the treasurership

he had raised his majority over Aneurin Bevan to more
than four million votes. He made use of the occasion of the
winding up to make a very full statement of his own personal
position. All those who were present will remember what a
remarkable speech it was. It showed the common-sense
approach to industrial matters which we in the trade unions
regarded as important, but it also showed the socialist vision
which was essential in a leader of the Labour Party. May I
quote just a few sentences from it:

> I would like to tell you, if I may, why I am a Socialist and have
> been for some 30 years. I became a Socialist quite candidly not
> so much because I was a passionate advocate of public ownership
> but because at a very early age I came to hate and loathe social
> injustice, because I disliked the class structure of our society,
> because I could not tolerate the indefensible difference of status
> and income which disfigures our society. I hated the insecurity
> that affected such a large part of our community while others
> led lives of security and comfort. I became a Socialist because I
> hated poverty and squalor.

The speech was followed by loud and prolonged applause.
Those who had obviously attacked him in the past for lack of
warmth and humanity were angry and discomforted. A num
ber walked out of the hall unable to bear the great reception
which Hugh Gaitskell was receiving.

This was early in October 1955. Two months later Mr.
Attlee resigned as leader of the Parliamentary Labour Party
and on 14 December 1955 Hugh Gaitskell was decisively
elected his successor.

Hugh Gaitskell did not grow up in the trade union movement, but from his early contact with the miners of Nottinghamshire as a University Extra Mural Tutor he understood
the purpose and approach of the unions. I always found that
he mixed easily at conference and was very ready to sit through
the most boring speeches. He did not have the arrogance

towards the trade unions which is sometimes associated with intellectuals in politics. I found him straightforward in all my dealings with him and with the basic loyalty which is essential to the unity and success of the Labour movement. He had much to contend with during his life-time, but he came through unscarred. In particular, he showed great courage in the year after the Scarborough conference in the face of outspoken public attacks. I did not always agree with him, but he always commanded my respect. He would have made a worthy Prime Minister.

2. Sam Watson

It was the early summer of 1954. Following a meeting of the National Executive Committee of the Labour Party I was sitting in the old Long Bar of the House of Commons when Aneurin Bevan came up to me and asked me to walk with him on the terrace. We went out into the sunshine and he raised immediately the question of the treasurership of the Labour Party, which had become vacant through the death of Arthur Greenwood. He asked if he could count on the miners' vote. I was obliged to tell him that the NUM had already decided that its nominee for the succession was Hugh Gaitskell. Bevan was very angry. 'How,' he asked, 'can you support a public schoolboy from Winchester against a man born in the back streets of Tredegar?' This was, on the face of it, a fair question. How was it that in the internal struggles in the Labour Party in the 1950s that many of the trade unions found themselves lined up in support of Hugh Gaitskell?

It would, of course, be foolish to say that Gaitskell was close to the trade unions if the implication of this is that the eight million trade unionists ever came to know him well. On the other hand, many of the leaders of the great trade unions— who are much more representative of the rank and file than they are often given credit for—did come to regard Hugh Gaitskell with considerable respect. Hugh Gaitskell never wooed the trade unions, but he won them nevertheless.

In challenging for the treasurership of the party Aneurin Bevan was in some ways a victim of his own dislike for Gaitskell. Gaitskell never spoke to me ungenerously about Bevan and he did not himself seek the treasurership in 1954. As an ex-Chancellor of the Exchequer he was already a major figure in the movement, but he was without a seat on the National Executive Committee. Bevan was also a major figure, but since 1946 he had regularly headed the constituency section in the annual elections to the NEC. The office of Treasurer carried no additional prestige: it was an attractive office only because it placed the encumbent on the NEC. Bevan would have been far wiser in 1954 to have acknowledged that Gaitskell deserved a place on the NEC and then to have conceded the treasurership to him.

I first heard of Hugh Gaitskell through Hugh Dalton in the early years of the war. I had joined Dalton on the NEC in 1941, but had seen a good deal of him previously as he was Member for Bishop Auckland in the County of Durham. He was at that time Minister of Economic Warfare, and Hugh Gaitskell was his personal assistant. Dalton spoke enthusiastically of Gaitskell as one of his young men. But he also spoke of Gaitskell as working *with*, not simply as working *for*, him. This was partly a measure of Dalton's generosity, but, in addition, a tribute to a talent already recognized.

In the autumn of 1947 Hugh Gaitskell succeeded Emanuel Shinwell as Minister of Fuel and Power. Shinwell had sat for a mining constituency since his defeat of Ramsay MacDonald at Seaham in 1935. It is not surprising that some of those who negotiated on behalf of the miners were a little suspicious of the new Minister and had doubts about the succession. In practice we found him entirely straightforward, never promising what he could not deliver. He did what he said he could do and was frank when he was unable to help. It was this quality which over the years impressed the leaders of the trade unions. Hugh was a man of great intellectual ability and integrity and devoted to the Labour Party. Whether he had been to public school or not was therefore irrelevant.

Hugh Gaitskell's contribution to international socialism has probably been under-estimated, but he gave more time to the problems of socialists in other countries than Attlee, Dalton or Bevin before him. He was patient and understanding and regularly attended meetings of the Socialist International. This is why I later found it difficult to understand the logic of his approach to the Common Market. I found myself bitterly opposed to him on this, although after his speech at Brighton in 1962 I had a very pleasant note from him and I think he was relieved to find that our basic friendship was not impaired by our disagreement.

His attitude to Clause 4 was partly influenced by his vision of the need to help socialist parties on the continent of Europe to put themselves into a position where they could win power again. In addition, he attached a symbolic importance to changing Clause 4, believing that in this way the Labour Party could be made to appeal to new, younger voters. He made up his mind to attack Clause 4 without consultation with the trade union leaders. When he told me of his intention I said that I thought that it was misjudged and unnecessary, but it was already too late to shift him in his opinion.

It is true that he was sometimes lacking in short-term political judgement. Nor was he always the best judge of men. There was a total absence of political calculation in his relationships with people and he sometimes failed to realize the extent to which a word or gesture from him would be appreciated. On the other hand he was more than ready to correct this fault if his attention was drawn to it.

An ability to work with people was certainly one of Hugh Gaitskell's qualities. He was prepared to make decisions and, as we all know, to take a stand. But he did not ride rough-shod over people or presume that he had a special status on committees on which he served. He was an effective committee man both for this reason and—judging from my experience of him on the NEC—because he always read his papers before a meeting, which few members of a committee do.

It is difficult now to look back on a relationship which I had come to take for granted. I discussed with Hugh Gaitskell all the major issues of the last ten years of his life, and we worked together closely on many of them. I had the task, for example, at the Scarborough conference of 1960, of opening the debate on unilateralism, which Hugh closed with his powerful and dramatic speech. Towards the end of 1962 I thought that he was looking tired and far from well, but this was hardly surprising after the strains of the previous years. I did not guess that his last illness was approaching. When Hugh visited Durham he always stayed at my home. I was expecting to see him many times again.

Hugh greatly enjoyed his visits to the Durham Miners' Gala. On the balcony outside the Royal County Hotel he was at his most benign as he watched the banners pass—almost like a teddy bear in his warmth and spontaneity. He was exactly the same when he met the staff of the hotel, as was customary after the official lunch. He was easy and friendly and always appeared to enjoy himself. He was much loved by the Durham miners and their wives.

Hugh Gaitskell came through a dark tunnel to the point where he was not only a party leader but a national figure with a world-wide reputation. The journey was often lonely and exhausting, but he always had a clear vision of the purpose for which he was in politics. He saw the extent to which the world was changing and, in particular, recognized the great revolution in technology as it was affecting the home and the factory and would affect the attitudes to the Labour Party as well. He became leader of the party at a time when it contained the seeds of possible disintegration into cliques and sectionalism but almost unaided he left it an army fit to conquer. In his much criticized Scarborough speech he declared his intention to 'fight and fight and fight again to save the party we love'. He did love the Labour Party and it stands now as a monument to his achievement.

LEADER OF THE OPPOSITION

Roy Jenkins

My friendship with Hugh Gaitskell, although it arose out of politics, was not primarily a political one. To a substantial extent it could, I think, have survived prolonged political disagreement or even complete separation. Yet the Gaitskell I knew was always a leading politician. When I first saw him he was already a departmental Minister. I have no clear recollection of speaking to him before he was Chancellor of the Exchequer. And during the years when I knew him best and saw him most frequently he was a highly dominant leader of the Opposition, living under the constant pressure of public events.

Unlike several of the other contributors to this volume, therefore, who knew him in much earlier days, I did not see Gaitskell develop from obscurity to fame. When I knew him he was always in the centre of events, and most of his triumphs and failures were political ones. But not all of them. At times he dominated politics. But he was rarely dominated by them. This was not primarily because of the range of his interests, although that was considerable, and not at all because he had any peculiar quality of unconcern; on the contrary he was easily emotionally involved. The true reason was the immensely high priority which he always gave to matters of personal relationship. He cared desperately about his friends, and the

small change of social intercourse assumed an unusual importance in his life. In the midst of a period of high success he could
be temporarily but deeply cast down by the unexpected failure
of some small private event to which he had been looking
forward. As a result, he conspicuously lacked that quality of
cool, tough, detachment from individual affections which is
often considered essential for a leading politician. He could be
blind to the faults of those whom he liked and equally blind to
the virtues of those he did not—and in neither case was he in the
least influenced by a calculation of who could be useful to him.
He would sometimes throw away political allies with an
extraordinary recklessness, yet he clung to personal friendship
with a persistent loyalty.

All this sounds like a recipe for careless and attractive
failure in politics. Yet Gaitskell was cheated of the highest
achievement only by the tragedy of his illness and death. Even
without its natural fulfilment, however, his life in politics was
one of outstanding success. At forty-nine he achieved the
leadership of a major party, and did so at a time when formidable rivals were thicker on the ground than they are today.
During the seven years for which he held this office he consistently opted for strong leadership. This was not a question of
the force of his personality, or of any desire to dominate. It was
simply that he believed it was his duty to make up his mind
before rather than after his followers. He always pointed the way
and asked them to follow. The result was that the Gaitskell era
was an adventurous one in Labour Party history. The leader
engaged in a continuous dialogue with the party of which he
was the head. But this, while it does not make for a calm life,
is the essence of strong democratic leadership. It is only then
that great changes in the outlook of a party or a nation can be
carried through. It is only then that a leader in opposition,
without the prospect of immediate office (and this was
Gaitskell's position during most of his seven-year tenure) can

make as great an impact as any minister upon opinion and events. This latter effect Gaitskell undoubtedly achieved. Mild-mannered ex-don though he may have appeared at the date of election, he became better known to the general public than any former leader of the opposition who had never been Prime Minister.

Both at the higher level of influencing events and at the lower one of household fame, therefore, Gaitskell, in spite of his lack of professionalism and his privately, rather than publicly, orientated personality, was a successful, even a memorable leader. What were the qualities which made him this, and how did they develop during the last decade of his life?

His first break-through to fame was when he became Chancellor of the Exchequer at the age of forty-four. This promotion came unexpectedly, almost casually. Previously he had been a quietly competent departmental minister and assistant to Cripps at the Treasury. His sudden elevation to one of the first three positions in the Government owed everything to the confidence of those with whom he had worked closely and almost nothing to his public standing. Even as Chancellor his public fame was limited. It was during the summer of 1951 that an incident, which he subsequently liked to relate, occurred in a London restaurant. Gaitskell was lunching with friends when a woman came across and asked if he would give her his autograph for her schoolboy son. By no means displeased, he smilingly obliged. 'Thank you very much,' she said. 'My son will be so pleased. You see, he has always wanted to be a lawyer, and he admires you more than almost anyone else, Sir Hartley.'

While he was at the Exchequer luck ran steadily against him. The government as a whole was tired. Its majority was tiny. The Korean War and the rearmament programme which followed from it brought vast economic difficulties. Aneurin Bevan, the most popular minister with the Labour Party activists, was restless and looking to the years of opposition which seemed to lie inevitably ahead. In these circumstances a young Chancellor, without any particular following of his own, might have been expected to play for safety. Instead, Gaitskell showed a determination verging on stubbornness. He emerged as the one strong man of the Labour Government's last year. He made enemies, but a public reputation as well.

When the Government went out, however, it looked as though his position might not hold. Nearly all the other leading figures in the Labour Party had experience in opposition. Gaitskell had none. Before the war he had been a don and during the war a Civil Servant. As a minister he might be very good, but surely he, more than most, worked best with the smooth support of the Whitehall machine and would be lost without it.

This prognosis proved to be the reverse of the truth. In office everything came easily to him and he was a moderate success. In opposition he had to fight a long, often disagreeable battle to establish his position, but he eventually stood out as the dominant politician of his generation.

First, he had to take the decision to compete. In Parliament this was easy enough. For a time, at any rate, his rôle there was secure. But it needed to be buttressed by a position in the party outside which he did not at that stage possess. That meant that he had to make a place for himself as a Labour Party conference figure. The temptation not to try for this— at any rate for a time—would for many people have been overwhelming. In 1952, the first year of opposition, with Bevanism firmly in the constituency saddle, the conference was much more a demonstration against the Right of the party than a deliberative assembly. In theory, Gaitskell could easily have stood aside. There have frequently been Labour ministers almost but not quite of the first rank, who have been active in Parliament, but have steered clear of the rougher arena of the party conference.

Gaitskell, however, was prevented from following this course by two factors. First, he could never bear to contract out of conflict. Perhaps surprisingly for a man of gentle manners and quiet charm, he was fascinated by it. He did not positively like rough interchanges and political in-fighting, as Ernest Bevin or Aneurin Bevan appeared to do, but he could not keep away from them. Morally, he was in the bravest of all categories: he flinched, but he always went on. He disliked the noise, but he never kept away from the place where the guns were firing loudest.

Second, he had a shrewd sense of power and realized that, without establishing a position in the conference, he could never achieve the commanding rôle in the Labour Party to which his other talents seemed to entitle him. Accordingly, in 1952, in the dismal resort of Morecambe and at the most bitter and snarling of all such assemblies, there began the curious love-hate relationship between Gaitskell and the Labour conference which was to dominate much of the rest of his life.

That year he was heavily defeated for the National Executive Committee. He followed this up by the challenge of his Stalybridge speech. This was delivered on his way back from Morecambe and seemed at the time to be an act of almost foolhardy defiance. Many were muttering that the Labour Party was slipping into an irresponsible extremism which would condemn it to a long period of sterility, and that Communist infiltration was doing much to stir up this mood. Gaitskell said in public these things which others were merely whispering. By so doing he make himself the most exposed man in the party, who looked for the moment as though he could never again be acceptable to the bulk of its opinion. Exposed, as prominences always are, he had certainly become, but he had also taken a big step towards becoming the recognized leader of that moderate section of the party, which, particularly as elections approach, almost always triumphs.

Henceforward, there could be no question of his being thought of as merely a 'technocratic' minister, a sort of substitute Civil Servant who had been pushed up quickly because he was good at running a department. He had become a political power in his own right.

In the meantime, Gaitskell was rapidly increasing his parliamentary stature. Butler was at the Exchequer and he was Shadow Chancellor. Although they were both accused of the besetting party sin of 'Butskellism', economic debates during this period were conducted at a higher level and with more interest on both sides than in any other period since the war. Gaitskell's annual reply to the Budget became a regular parliamentary *tour de force*, listened to with rapt attention by a packed House. For the first time in these speeches there was shown to the full those qualities which became characteristic of his parliamentary oratory at its best: a very full knowledge of the subject, presented with a relentless logic, which avoided aridity because of the emotional force, never shrill or bitter, which lay behind it. In addition, I think that, at this time, he had a more successful and more frequently applied lighter touch than in later years.

During this first period of opposition it was also possible to see Gaitskell's quality of leadership, exercised at first on a fairly intimate stage. Still very much an economic specialist, he worked closely with a group of four or five lieutenants, one or two of whom had distinctly uncompromising personalities. Private relations were very close amongst the group, and Gaitskell could be treated with as much mocking but friendly disrespect as anyone else. But in matters of work his authority was effortless. Everyone would undertake tasks because he wanted them done, and enjoyed doing them under his direction. He could build up loyalty by the imposition of burdens.

Outside Parliament, Gaitskell's position remained uncertain until the autumn of 1954. In 1953 he was again defeated for the party executive. It began to look as though he and Aneurin Bevan had settled down to the boring attrition of trench warfare. From his emplacement with the constituency parties Bevan kept up a fairly constant bombardment of Gaitskell's equally well dug-in position with the parliamentary party; and vice versa. But it was not an exchange which seemed likely to produce a decisive result. Then the Treasurership of the Labour Party fell vacant. For this post, unimportant in itself, the whole conference, trades unions as well as constituency parties, elects. Both contestants were given an opportunity to get out of their trenches and they both responded with alacrity. The result was a clear victory for Gaitskell. The majority of the big trade union leaders had decided that Gaitskell, despite his utterly dissimilar background from their own, was a man with whom they could work, and that Bevan was not. The decision came at a most important stage in his career.

After this result there was a gradual ebbing of the ideological conflict within the party. The General Election of 1955 contributed towards this, but even when it had been lost, there was no return to the full bitterness of the preceding years. 'Bevanism' was on the wane, and several of its most intelligent adherents were beginning to seek other rôles. At the 1955 conference the old lines of dispute were much less in evidence, and Gaitskell surprised his audience, many of whom had been conditioned to think of him as 'a desiccated calculating machine', with a strong declaration of his basic political beliefs. For the first time he began to acquire a hold on the emotions of the party.

That year Attlee was clearly near to relinquishing his twenty-year-old leadership. Gaitskell came only gradually and reluctantly to accept the view that he ought to be a candidate. This was not out of mock modesty. I do not think he doubted, at that stage, that he would one day be party leader. But, at forty-nine, he believed that Herbert Morrison, with whom he had worked closely over the preceding five years,

should have a turn first. In June 1955, he argued most deter-
minedly in favour of this course. Over the summer, however,
he was persuaded that the desire of the Labour MPs was for a
much younger leader than Morrison. If he allowed him to be
the only 'moderate' candidate, Bevan might conceivably still
snatch a victory; and even if he did not, a short Morrison
tenure might lead to a subsequent reaction in favour of
the Left.

Once he was convinced of the force of these arguments
Gaitskell went forward unhesitatingly. He told Morrison of
his decision at the earliest possible moment in October, choos-
ing a luncheon with no one else present—not perhaps the
easiest occasion—for breaking the news. He certainly did
not look forward to doing so, and when it was over he
was greatly relieved. Morrison had taken the information remarkably well. Perhaps at this stage it was natural
tolerance. Perhaps he underestimated the force of Gaitskell's
challenge. If the latter was the case, he was greatly mistaken.
When the contest came, in December, Gaitskell swept the
field. He was elected on the first ballot, with nearly twice as
many votes as the combined total of Morrison and Bevan.
He was the youngest leader of any party for sixty years.

Suez was Gaitskell's first crisis in his new position. At
first he seemed to hesitate, but as soon as he saw that Lord Avon
intended to seek a solution through force, Gaitskell mounted an
impassioned denunciation of his actions. He carried most of
the Labour Party—and many others—enthusiastically with him
on this course. But there were a few Labour MPs who stood
more or less quietly aside, and it was noticeable—a piquant
situation—that Aneurin Bevan was much less whole-hearted
in his condemnation of the Government's adventure.

Superficially Gaitskell's reaction may have been surprising.
He was not particularly sympathetic to the Nasserite régime,
and he had been opposed to the method by which it had taken

over the Canal. Nor was he, as the chief supporter of the 1951 rearmament programme, in any way sympathetic to pacifism or backward in the legitimate defence of British interests. But his whole outlook at that stage, and for all but a very brief period of his life, was instinctively internationalist. He believed deeply in the Western Alliance and in friendship with the United States. He was naturally a mid-Atlantic man, almost as much at home in New York as in London. The rôle which he sought for Britain was that of a loyal ally, not of a maverick power chasing off irresponsibly on her own. He cared greatly too about our standing in the United Nations. He had a high respect for the institution and for world public opinion. He had always been willing to stand against Soviet aggression, and he was revolted by the thought that we had reduced ourselves to their level. Equally, he was inclined to favour a bi-partisan foreign policy, and was the more resentful of Eden for, as he saw it, shattering the basis of this than were others who, always believing the Tories were wrong, had no store of surplus indignation to use against them.

Gaitskell's vehemence on this issue, widely criticized though it was, even by some who were themselves opposed to the Government's action, probably did him no harm in the country. It helped to imprint his personality upon the public, and it began a period in which the Labour Party bounded ahead of the Conservatives in the public opinion polls. Where it did do him some harm was in the House of Commons. For some months afterwards he had difficulty in getting a good hearing from the Government benches. Their occupants paid him back with mocking noise for his part in the destruction of Eden. It was an experience to which he was most unused and which was peculiarly upsetting to his style of oratory. It caused him great concern, which I remember him expressing to me in May 1957. When would this derision end, and if it did not, could he continue to be an effective leader of the opposition?

In fact it ended very soon, and Gaitskell never again had the least difficulty in exercising a full command over the House. What was perhaps a more permanent legacy of Suez was that this naturally moderate statesman was never afterwards on really good terms with the leader of the Conservative Party. With Eden until Suez he got on well enough. But their easy relationship did not survive the clash. And with Macmillan he was always on terms of armed hostility. It seems unlikely that either understood or respected the other. What Macmillan thought of Gaitskell we do not know, but what Gaitskell thought of Macmillan, above all, was that he cheated at politics. His own reckless honesty, accompanied by a compulsive desire to set out every argument in terms which were logically convincing (but sometimes emotionally provocative) made him disdainful of Macmillan's fondness for doing everything behind a smoke-screen. Only, perhaps, in the last weeks before his illness did Gaitskell begin to develop a somewhat warmer feeling for the Prime Minister.

With his principal rivals within the Labour Party, however, Gaitskell's relations improved rapidly in the period after Suez. Wilson had already succeeded him as Shadow Chancellor. Bevan was at first a little more recalcitrant. But at the Brighton conference of 1957 his 'naked into the conference chamber' speech led both to a rupture with his old friends of the uni-lateralist Left and to a reconciliation with Gaitskell. Shortly afterwards Gaitskell asked him to become Shadow Foreign Secretary and the relationship between the two men became amicable and moderately close. It reached its high-water mark during their joint visit to Russia immediately preceding the 1959 General Election. Power seemed near, and Bevan appeared satisfied with his prospective rôle as Foreign Secretary. Gaitskell was happy to see him fill it in a big way. Not the least of his achievements of leadership was that, for a time, he acquired the knack of working closely with Bevan's rumbustious but magnetic personality, and of harnessing its force without hiding himself beneath its shadow.

This important partnership was first made less relevant by the election defeat, and then destroyed by Bevan's sudden illness and subsequent death. The election campaign, on the whole skilfully fought by Gaitskell (although he was subsequently critical of himself for one major mistake), was hard throughout and at the end cruelly disappointing. Before it began he had been cautious about victory. Until the last six months or so of the Parliament it had looked as though the Government could hardly hope to recover. Then the public opinion polls had begun to swing and Gaitskell had half reconciled himself to this new outlook. Throughout the campaign itself, however, he was consistantly buoyant. He generated confidence by effort and swept others along with him. His confidence was not a façade. Twelve days before polling he told me that he was sure of a Labour victory, and remained so, I believe, until the returns began to come in. The disappointment was therefore as sudden as it was heavy.

His hopes died in the Leeds City Hall, with the television cameras frequently upon him. As the Conservative gains mounted previously dammed-up waves of tiredness rolled over him, and as they did so he faced the prospect, not of the period of constructive power for which he was perfectly poised at the time, but of the unavoidable bickering of a three times defeated party. One was inevitably reminded of Adlai Stevenson's, 'It hurts too much to laugh, and I'm too old to cry'. Yet if he did not laugh, Gaitskell at least managed to smile, slowly and a little sadly, as he so often did, when with a quiet grace he conceded defeat.

Looking back, this defeat was unavoidable. No radical leader could have carried the country in its 1959 mood. Gaitskell did at least as well as anyone else would have done. But the inevitability was not so obvious as the time. The whole

Labour Party began to cast about for the causes of the setback. From the moment of his return to London, Gaitskell was active in the search. Perhaps mistakenly, he allowed himself no period of recuperation. Without doubt, he and those of us who were close to him, made serious tactical mistakes during the ensuing weeks. We over-estimated the rationality of political movements. Equally without doubt, however, the battle which then began, and continued, in different phases, for two years, had to be fought. Broadly the Labour Party was divided into two camps. On the one side stood those who wished to react to defeat by giving the party a more modern appearance and a stronger appeal to the uncommitted voter. They saw its essential rôle as that of providing an effective alternative government to the Conservatives. It must therefore appeal to the marginal members of the Leftward thinking half of the country.

On the other side stood those whose primary concern was to defend the ideological citadel. If the citadel became increasingly cut off from the surrounding countryside and unpopular with the inhabitants that could not be helped. Elections were not of primary importance. One prominent socialist thinker wrote cheerfully of another ten years of Conservative government.

Some members of the party stood a little apart from both the camps, and it would have been theoretically possible for Gaitskell to have joined them. But it would have been utterly out of keeping with both his character and his convictions. He was incapable of equating a leader's rôle with that of a chairman.

The first phase of the battle—that over Clause 4—was far from an immediate success. Gaitskell and those who were with him tried to move an injured party into a more comfortable position, and were rewarded for their efforts with some sharp and angry cries. Even so they got it a little way, before the attempt had to be abandoned. Yet, after this abandonment and the shifting of attention away from the issue, the party began quietly and almost imperceptibly to move itself in the direction indicated. No one looking at the programme, outlook and assumptions of the Labour Party today could doubt that Gaitskell, in a long-term sense, had won his battle. The party is incomparably closer to what he wanted than to what his opponents wanted. It would not go the whole way at his bidding. But it would not have gone at all had he not taken the risk of pointing the way.

After the Clause 4 stalemate came the counter-attack. It was on another front, that of unilateralism and neutralism *versus* the commitment to the Atlantic alliance and the defence policy which this entailed. But basically it was the same issue— whether the Labour Party's rôle was to be primarily that of a party of power or a party of protest. During the spring and summer of 1960 the unilateralist forces built up with frightening speed. Union after union toppled almost casually into their camp. Gaitskell's position became more exposed than that of any party leader since Baldwin in 1930.

At the Scarborough conference that autumn the almost unthinkable happened. On the central policy issue of the year the leadership was defeated. It had nearly—but not quite— occurred over German rearmament in 1954, and everyone had then assumed that an adverse vote would be an intolerable humiliation for Lord Attlee, rendering his continuance in office almost impossible. Yet he was less committed on that issue than his successor was on unilateralism.

What, then, would Scarborough mean for Gaitskell? Would it force his resignation, or would it leave him with the possibility of carrying on only as the prisoner of a section of his 'followers', a figure shown to be so weak that he could not hope to command respect in the House or in the country? In fact, by one of the odd quirks of history, Gaitskell avoided both these alternatives by the widest possible margin. Even the conference itself was far from being a humiliation for him, although it was a great emotional strain. A majority of the delegates was committed to vote against him, but by the time the crucial debate took place many of them were regretting their mandates.

Gaitskell, in his own speech, had both to capitalize this mood and to raise a banner around which men would fight, if necessary risking their political positions in the process. Typically, he chose to do this in the least equivocal way possible. There was no doubt about his banner; the doubt was whether the men with uneasy minds would follow it.

This last doubt was soon removed. His old bastion of the Parliamentary Labour Party remained reasonably secure. When Harold Wilson hesitantly decided to run against him for the leadership his majority was more than two-to-one. And as the contest was fought on the clear understanding that Gaitskell, if successful, would lead against the Scarborough decision, the result struck a great blow, not only against the decision, but against the whole principle of conference authority. Yet he could not rest on this victory. Throughout that winter of 1960-1, Gaitskell 'fought, fought and fought again' on innumerable platforms up and down the country. Nearly every week-end he would make three or four full-length speeches. His physical resilience appeared as high as ever, and he would often fortify himself with a late evening of relaxed conversation before setting out on these grinding expeditions; but, in fact, he was near the margin of his strength.

Sometimes at these meetings the reception would be hostile and even noisy. In these circumstances one of Gaitskell's greatest strengths was his stubborn faith in the power of reasoned argument. What he prided himself upon being was a rational man. The superiority of the multi-lateralist case was to him so obvious that intelligent people of good-will must

surely see it. He would go on patiently explaining what he
believed until others believed it too. And this approach,
combined with his immense agreeableness of manner in
friendly intercourse, succeeded in shifting a good deal of opinion within the party. But was it shifting fast enough? As
the Easter union conferences approached this looked extremely
uncertain. Gaitskell suddenly began to foresee the prospect of a
second defeat, and to recognize that this might be fatal. For
a party leader to defy a single conference aberration was one
thing. For him to attempt to ignore a series of adverse decisions,
amounting to the expression of a settled point of view, was
something quite different.

At this stage, more I think than at Scarborough, Gaitskell
faced in his own mind the distinct likelihood that in six months'
time he might have to go—probably to retire completely from
politics. It was a discouraging prospect. It would mean that his
period as a party leader, which had begun under such bright
auspices just over five years before, would end in complete
failure. He would be remembered only as the man who led his
party to its third successive electoral defeat and was then
rejected by his own followers. Once he had assimilated this
possibility in his mind, he faced it with complete equanimity.

Then, with bewildering rapidity, the outlook changed.
When it was least expected an avalanche movement began. The
unions followed each other back into the Gaitskell camp as
quickly as, the year before, they had moved the other way.
Many of the constituency parties did the same. All the hard
persuasive work of the winter began to bear simultaneous
fruit.

The victory which this made certain was ratified at Blackpool
in October 1961. It left Gaitskell in a far stronger position than
he had been before Scarborough. He was dominant in the
Labour Party, and he had impressed the public outside as a
leader of force, wisdom and courage. No one foresaw that

he had only fifteen months of leadership ahead. By his efforts he seemed to have secured for himself a long tenure of the leadership on conditions of tolerable authority. But what in fact he had done was to bequeath this easement to his successor, and to give Harold Wilson the elbow-room which has helped him to look like a Prime Minister. If Gaitskell had lost, not only himself but any other Labour leader for years to come would have paid part of the price.

The use to which Gaitskell himself put the new room for manœuvre was, ironically, a most unwelcome one to many of his closest supporters on previous issues. He swung the Labour Party into a posture of general hostility towards Britain joining the Common Market. The merits of this issue need not be argued here. I would merely record that while his attitude here seemed to me not wholly consistent with his previous general outlook on world affairs, it was in no way the result of a sudden lurch, taken with electoral considerations heavily in mind. I had seen his opposition growing for a year or more before it finally revealed its full force to the public. Like all his political positions it was fixed partly by logic and partly by emotion. And once fixed, he held to it with great tenacity.

I then had the opportunity (although it was a small con- solation at the time) to see his political qualities and defects through, as it were, the other end of the telescope. Broadly, they looked much the same as I had previously thought them to be, although I inevitably felt a little more sympathy with those who had so often differed from him in the past. Courage could be interpreted as inflexibility and an aggressive respect for rationality as a tendency to equate little points and big ones. Yet, by and large, he appeared just as impressive as a temporary opponent as he had so long done as an ally and leader. The warm persuasiveness of his manner and the absolute honesty of his purpose were formidable weapons, on whichever side of them one stood.

Nor did this difference make close personal relations with him impossible. At first I thought it would, but that was under the shock of a sudden break in a long habit of agreement. But then he made it clear that he was still faithful to his old rule of the primacy of private relations. For the last few weeks of his active life we were back on terms of the closest friendship.

What did he leave to English politics? First, the promise of being a great Prime Minister, not because he would necessarily have avoided mistakes, but because he would have infused the whole Government with a sense of loyalty and purpose, and made men of widely differing gifts and character proud to serve under him. Second, a Labour Party with both the will and the capacity for victory, two qualities of which, without him, it might only too easily have deprived itself. And third, a memory which is a standing contradiction to those who wish to believe that only men with cold hearts and twisted tongues can succeed in politics.

Cartoon by Vicky from the *News Chronicle*, 20 October, 1950

1. As a child he spent some time in Burma where his father was a Civil Servant

2. In England he stayed with relatives

3. At six he went to the Dragon school at Oxford where he made friendships that lasted all his life

4. As a boy at Winchester he was not particularly happy, but at Oxford he found his feet, working hard and enjoying himself, as at this OUDS ball. His sister, Dorothy, is second from the right. He is in the harlequin costume

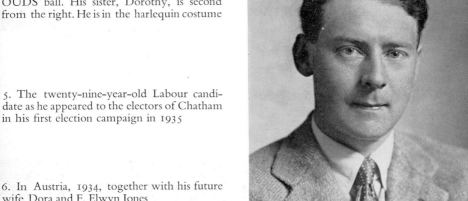

5. The twenty-nine-year-old Labour candidate as he appeared to the electors of Chatham in his first election campaign in 1935

6. In Austria, 1934, together with his future wife Dora and F. Elwyn Jones

7. From the 1926 General Strike onwards he had a close association with the coal industry, but it was as Minister of Fuel and Power, 1947-50, that he won the confidence of the miners' unions. He is seen here underground at a Yorkshire pit

8. He was forty-four when he succeeded Stafford Cripps as Chancellor of the Exchequer in 1950. He was forced to grapple in his 1951 Budget with the severe consequences of the Korean War

9. Jersey, 1951, with his wife and daughters, Julia (right) and Cressida. He drew much strength from the affection of his close family circle

10. He enjoyed social functions of all kinds, particularly when they provided an opportunity for dancing, as did this Labour Party reception in 1956

1. Together with the Prime Minister, Harold Macmillan, his principal opponent
in the House of Commons for six years, he received an honorary degree at
Oxford in 1958

2. After the bitter arguments of the early 1950s, relations with Aneurin Bevan
greatly improved during Bevan's period as Shadow Foreign Secretary. They are
seen here in 1959 with Erich Ollenhauer, Chairman of the German Social
Democratic Party

13. On several occasions he and his family took a holiday in Yugoslavia. He met President Tito both socially and to discuss international problems

14. The year following the 1960 Scarborough conference saw the gruelling fight against unilateralism. Occasionally there were ugly scenes at meetings he addressed, like this one in Hyde Park on May Day 1961

15. During busy years as a Minister and then, later, as Leader of the Opposition he continued to make regular visits to Leeds to deal with constituency problems. In the 1959 General Election he held his seat with a large majority, but in the country as a whole Labour lost heavily

16. His last major speech, on the Common Market at the 1962 Brighton conference, was one of his greatest, and finally consolidated his leadership. He is seen here at Brighton with Harold Wilson, who was to succeed him as leader, and George Brown, deputy leader of the Labour Party (left)

17. This was his room in his home at 18 Frognal Gardens, London

THE DIVISION OF EUROPE

Willy Brandt

In September 1955, at a meeting arranged in Milan by the
Congress for Cultural Freedom, Hugh Gaitskell spoke about
'The Future of Economic Growth'. His address on the changed
approach to the problem since the time when, as a young
political economist, he had been obliged to concern himself
with the 'cancer of unemployment' was listened to most atten-
tively. But if I say that our attention was concentrated even
more on the personality of the presumed future leader of the
Labour Party, this does not detract from his intellectual achievement. Not long after he did become Leader of Her Majesty's
Opposition.

In March 1957 I met him again in Berlin; he had undertaken
to give an Ernst Reuter Lecture in the main lecture hall of
our Free University. At that time I was a member of the
Bundestag and President of the Berlin House of Representatives; I was elected Mayor a few months later. On the evening
before Hugh Gaitskell's lecture I sat in his company. We did
not agree on all points, but I was deeply impressed by the
nobility of his character, the breadth of his outlook, and the
power of his mind. The next day he gave us a very clear
and simple exposé of his political convictions. He believed, he
told us, that parliamentary democracy was the most tolerable

kind of political system that had so far been discovered. But he believed in addition that in the social sphere there must be justice and equality for all, without discrimination on racial, religious, or social grounds. 'We should enshrine these ideals,' he said 'in our law-making and administration. We recognize that not everyone can see eye to eye with us, that people have a right to their own opinion and the right to advocate it. We should recognize that democracy depends on tolerance, and on the goodwill of the members of a community towards each other.' He expressly added that he was a realist, especially in judging communist philosophy and communist aims.

This was the period shortly after the revolution in Hungary and the changes in Poland. Gaitskell gathered hope from these events. What had happened in these two countries made him suspect—and here we were in full agreement with him—that the demand and passionate longing for freedom had not been destroyed by the terror and propaganda of the communists. The intellectuals had not become robots, and, above all, decisive forces from amongst young people were rising against the dictatorship. In the Soviet Union, too, a change, he thought, was taking place. One should not be over-optimistic or assume that democratization was already under way, but there was, none the less, a certain easing. He considered a simple return to rigid Stalinist politics unlikely.

Gaitskell was already then posing the question of a real co-existence in the sense of the elimination of the causes of tension. Among these causes he included above all the division of Germany and the Russian hegemony over Eastern Europe; as a democrat one certainly could not be content with that. But he explained that these problems could not be solved by force. The idea of neutralizing Germany he regarded as dangerous. Nor did he believe that it could be taken for granted that the Russians would accept proposals for disengagement in Central Europe in the current situation. But he contemplated that it would be possible to negotiate solutions of this kind in years to come, so as to reach a solution of the German problem as well.

What he set himself passionately against was the danger of a political and diplomatic 'Maginot Line mentality' in the Western camp. He set himself against the passiveness of the West, against its readiness to yield up the initiative to the Russians: 'that would mean simply and solely pursuing a policy of being ready to defend ourselves by force of arms, while considering the *status quo* as something unavoidable about which nothing could be done.' He thought the time had come to leave the initiative no longer entirely to the Russians, but to start a specifically Western peace offensive.

Such notions were outdated by the Kruschev offensive that began late in 1957 and reached a climax at the end of 1958 with the Berlin ultimatum. But does this mean that they were wrong? Did they not acquire new topical interest at the very time when Hugh Gaitskell passed away? Does not the question of Western initiatives confront us more urgently than ever? Are not the ideas that preoccupied Gaitskell and others being taken up in American policy?

When I came to London in March 1958 as Mayor of Berlin, we hardly discussed these great issues. Together with a group of friends, we dined in the evening at the House of Commons. I reported on Berlin and other German matters. Gaitskell was worried, like me, about the credulity or thoughtlessness of some of his Parliamentary colleagues who enjoyed travelling in the Soviet zone of Germany. There are two other things I still remember clearly about that evening. First, the representatives of the Labour Party, with the Leader at their head, were decidedly confident about the result of the coming elections. Secondly, they talked about their hope of closer contact between Labour and the German Social Democrats. Co-operation between the two largest social-democratic parties of Europe had to be extended, though Gaitskell always included the Scandinavians in these considerations—he regarded me as half-Scandinavian, something which I did not mind! Those I talked with in London saw good possibilities for the shape of the future in such collaboration.

Then, in April 1959, we were both guests of the Swedish Prime Minister, Tage Erlander, at Harpsund, his country seat. Directly afterwards we celebrated seventy years of Swedish social democracy, in Stockholm. Of those who took part, the Danish Prime Minister, H. C. Hansen, and the President of the Socialist International, Alsing Andersen, passed away even before Hugh Gaitskell. Others joining in the talks were the Chairman of the German party, Erich Ollenhauer, the Austrian Foreign Minister Bruno Kreisky, and the President of the Finnish Parliament, Karl-August Fagerholm.

In the idyllic atmosphere—despite the rainy April weather —of Harpsund, Hugh Gaitskell's thoughts undoubtedly centred on the ever-approaching elections. I recall how he was badgered at a press conference about the financing of the budget and how much he was counting on the growth of the British economy to meet increased expenditure.

My own mind was, of course, more on the deadly serious problems that had been posed by the Berlin ultimatum of November 1958, at first due to expire after six months. There was much confusion in those days. Gaitskell, however, was among those who considered the defence of Western rights to be essential—not only for the sake of the people of Berlin, but because of everything else that would otherwise go downhill.

Along with Hugh Gaitskell, my wife and I flew to London in that April of 1959. In the House of Commons I had a very intimate conversation with Gaitskell and Aneurin Bevan, during which the latter expressed his grave fears over the possible consequences of a separate 'peace treaty' between

Moscow and East Berlin. Apart from the official programme of my visit, I was able to present my own view of the Berlin crisis to the Labour Party Executive and a great many MPs.

A few months later, in July 1959, I met Gaitskell and Bevan again, at the Congress of the Socialist International in Hamburg. What else could I do but speak once more of my distressed and threatened city? I again found that my British friends were behind me on the vital issues.

At the next Congress of the Socialist International—at Rome in October 1961—we had to settle an apparent dispute. I had come from an election campaign that brought my party two million extra votes, but no governmental responsibility. I had come from Berlin where very recently the Wall of Shame had been built, and which was having to endure another hard test of nerve. Gaitskell had helped prepare for the Congress of Rome an important supplement to the Declaration of Democratic-Socialist Principles. He had also undertaken to review the political situation of the world. There were certain of his ideas I could not agree with, above all for the partial recognition of the East German régime. But we were completely at one over the protection of Western rights and duties in Berlin; and Gaitskell was prepared to take a big risk for them. In spite of a few differences of opinion, our parties agreed on a joint resolution.

Hugh Gaitskell was staying with Italian friends in historic surroundings. I visited him there, and he told me he would come to Berlin as soon as possible. He came early in January 1962. At a small gathering we had a frank and friendly talk. He saw the Wall, and he saw what we were striving to achieve despite all our difficulties.

On 8 January, 1962 he said in the Berlin Congress Hall that he had had the experience 'of looking at a prison wall'. And he asked: 'Even if it is all one to Herr Ulbricht what sort of impression it makes, can Mr. Kruschev really be happy about creating such a devastating picture of Communism? To the Soviet government, that artist in propaganda, the prison wall must be an almost unbearable embarrassment.' Our British guest had satisfied himself that there were obviously worries about the future in West Berlin, but no lack of confidence and certainly no panic. He supported the Allies in their united resolve to stay in Berlin, and at the same time declared himself in favour of negotiations. In doing so he called it absurd to equate a readiness to negotiate with a readiness to give way. The second part of the address, which had been arranged by the German-English Society, dealt with the rôle and potentialities of the United Nations. One of his main points was that the remains of colonialism should be got rid of as quickly as possible.

After that we met several more times during 1962. I had received an invitation to make a number of speeches in Britain at the end of March. The first was to take place, after an introduction by Hugh Gaitskell, at Friends House in London. I had decided to plead the cause of a peaceful and liberal Germany. But even before it was my turn to speak, Gaitskell had trouble in getting a hearing, on account of the hecklers whom he dubbed 'communists and fascists'. Afterwards, however, the meeting was wound up in an orderly fashion, despite all efforts to interrupt it. Harold Wilson made the closing speech. Gaitskell told me that quite a large group of Labour MPs would shortly be coming to Berlin under Wilson's leadership. They did so, to our mutual benefit. But previously I had again seen Hugh Gaitskell at a luncheon to which Lord Home had invited us. And I sensed how embarrassing it was to him that I had encountered embarrassment at Friends House. Yet personally it had not troubled me at all, for I could only be astonished that a few muddled minds should try to make me out a Nazi. What did worry me was the relationship between our peoples—and our governments.

During the late autumn of 1962, I was once more in London,

in connection with an exhibition on Berlin and a concert given by our Philharmonic Orchestra. This was after the Cuba crisis, which changed so many things. It was also after Hugh Gaitskell's Labour Party conference speech about the European question, a speech that disappointed some of his friends on the Continent. In spite of many other engagements, Mrs. Gaitskell and he attended a reception at the German Embassy. The following day we had a final, intimate talk.

I knew him well enough, he said, not to take him for an anti-European. After all, everyone was aware, for example, of what he had done as Minister of State at the Treasury to bring the European Payments Union into being. All concerned would also know that there had never before been a Labour leader with such strong ties with the Continent. But he also had to stand up for the conditions he had formulated with regard to Britain's entry into the Common Market. He was pleased to hear from me that the German Social Democrats did not want to leave the other members of EFTA in the lurch. We also discussed a new Harpsund conference, which Walter Reuther and I had agreed on a few weeks earlier in Washington—and which took place only a few months later in different circumstances.

On 18 January, 1963, the Berlin Social Democrats opened their election campaign in the Deutschlandhalle. Friends from various European countries brought their greetings. Christopher Mayhew had come from London. We warmly applauded him when he spoke of the good wishes of many people for the gravely ill leader of his party. And then, at the end of that great meeting, came the shattering news that Hugh Gaitskell was dead. Tears came to our eyes, and we could say nothing. Someone had gone of whom not just his own people but all of us had expected so much. A statesman of distinction had left us, a wise man and a good friend.

ATTITUDES TOWARDS AMERICA

Arthur Schlesinger, Jnr.

The career of Hugh Gaitskell is remarkable in contemporary politics. Though the highest office he held in his own land was Chancellor of the Exchequer, he embodied the abiding values of democratic socialism—the commitment to social responsibility, justice and freedom—with such force and, at the same time, with such consideration for the views and values of others, that he became a central figure in the international democratic dialogue. This was a long growth. But the salient elements of his life—his education, his intellectual discipline, his early devotion to the Labour Party, his associations with the anti-Nazi underground in Vienna, his war-time work— all prepared him for this rôle. If death denied him the highest political opportunity in his own land, he still came to achieve an exceptional influence not only in Great Britain but throughout the democratic world.

I had, of course, known of Hugh Gaitskell for years, but I did not meet him until September 1955 at a conference in Milan under the sponsorship of the Congress for Cultural Freedom. As a result of war-time accidents, my first friends in the Labour Party were in the left wing. I had come to know Aneurin Bevan in 1944, when I lived in Eaton Place around the corner from the house he and Jennie Lee occupied with such liveliness and style in Cliveden Terrace, and I had been long under the spell of his audacious wit, melodious voice and sardonic-poetic imagination. Nonetheless, I had also been long aware of the fact that, much as I admired Aneurin Bevan, and much as I was beguiled by him, a philosophic gulf separated us. Nye Bevan had a precise and concrete response to precise and concrete stimuli. But he joined this to a comprehensive, abstract and ideological political sensibility. He liked Americans, but his theory of the United States, it always seemed to me, had been prematurely crystallized by youthful exposure to Jack London and Upton Sinclair. There seemed deep in him the feeling that any society founded in private ownership, no matter how diversified and agreeable its outward manifestations, was essentially wicked, and that any society founded on public ownership, no matter how cruel and arbitrary its outward manifestations, was potentially good. In practice, this feeling was always being challenged and defeated by hard facts, which, as a realistic and creative politician, he was prepared to recognize. But in the late evening ideology would control his conversation and colour his attitude.

I had supposed that the Labour Party must have its pragmatic as well as its evangelical strains, and I therefore met Hugh Gaitskell with particular interest. My first impression from Milan was that Gaitskell was a long way from being the 'desiccated calculating machine' of left-wing polemics. On the contrary, he seemed a man of unusual vitality, gaiety and charm. If he had a narrower cultural range than Bevan, who combined an intense interest in the arts with his ideological conception of politics, he had a wider human range. He did not allow ideology—or ego—to impede his understanding of human values or human predicaments. He was profoundly committed to a vision of a socialist Britain; but he interpreted, or reinterpreted, socialism in terms, not of structural absolutes, but of human possibilities.

I was bound to approach the Labour Party from the view-point of Franklin Roosevelt's New Deal, which had formed my own youthful political experience. Roosevelt had come to office in 1933 at a time when, under the stress of depression, the world had seemed to face a harsh choice between *laissez-faire* capitalism and totalitarian socialism. The issue was whether democratic government could possibly deal with mass unemployment—or rather whether the 'ruling forces' in capitalist society would permit democratic government to take the measures in social control and economic redistribution necessary to avert revolution. The experience of the MacDonald government in Great Britain had seemed to substantiate the case of those who declared there was no middle way. In 1931 Harold Laski gave the series of lectures at the University of North Carolina which later became the book, *Democracy in Crisis*. In theory, he said, the capitalists might co-operate in their own liquidation; but, if this were to happen, 'it is only necessary to say that it envisages something entirely new in historic experience'. The next year in *The State in Theory and Practice* Laski mocked the notion that one could build 'a *via media* between capitalism and socialism directed by the state in the interests of the whole community but without any change in the essential structure of class-relations'. Soon Laski would invoke the example of the MacDonald government to show that 'if socialists wish to secure a state built upon the principles of their faith, they can only do so by revolutionary means'. It was at this time that even Sir Stafford Cripps could write, 'The one thing that is not inevitable now is gradualness.'

The whole point of the New Deal was to reject this either/or approach to the economic problem, to affirm the possibilities of peaceful social evolution, and to deny the bleak dogmatism which argued that modern society had no alternative between *laissez-faire* and the total state. In seeking the *via media*, the United States had the advantage of Roosevelt's experimental genius, governed always by concern with human beings rather than with ideologies. In due course, it had too the aid of Keynesian economics. And, if the New Deal never succeeded in solving the problem of mass unemployment in the United States, it did succeed in inventing a variety of instruments and policies which suggested that men might achieve a society which united a tolerable diversity of ownership, a tolerable degree of freedom and a tolerable measure of economic growth.

The tableau of the 'thirties—the favourable example of the New Deal, the increasingly depressing example of the Soviet Union, and the liberating proposals of Keynes—had its impact on British socialism: it can be traced most compactly and lucidly in the writings of John Strachey. This process compelled a re-examination of the facile premises of classical socialism—a re-examination in which Hugh Gaitskell's friend Evan Durbin played a significant rôle. And it created the possibility that the future of mankind might lie, not with the ideologists, the apostles of either/or, but with the pragmatists, who sought through innovation and experiment to meet specific human needs.

Gaitskell plainly felt that classical socialism had lost a good deal of its relevance in the modern world. If socialism were to survive and prosper, he believed that it had to take the postwar realities into account. In domestic policy, this meant a world where the mixed economy, the welfare state, and the compensatory budget had shown that there were more roads to growth, equality, and justice than Marx—or Keir Hardie—had supposed. In foreign policy, this meant a world where communism was, not the ally of social democracy, but its mortal antagonist. His mission was, in a sense, the modernization of British socialism to deal with the real problems of the real world. He carried out this mission with passion, perseverance and authority.

It was a difficult mission. By the 1950s the Labour Party had become the most conservative party in Britain, at least in the sense that it had changed its ideas less in the preceding half-century than either the Liberals or the Tories. The constituency parties contained many men of evangelical zeal, irrevocably wedded to cherished platitudes. The left wing of the party was alert to spot all signs of revisionism or dilution. The right wing of the country liked modern socialism no better than it did classical socialism. None the less, Gaitskell seized the challenge of education and leadership. He tried to move beyond the old clichés to identify the new problems of the post-war world, and to devise new programmes and new policies. In some cases—as in Clause Four and in the Campaign for Nuclear Disarmament—there seemed no alternative to a frontal attack. Neither his courage nor his energy faltered; and, amidst occasional loneliness and discouragement, he kept up the fight.

In the end, he won. To examine the programme of the Labour Party today is to measure his success. The platitudes and clichés have to a considerable degree faded away. Austerity is regarded as a condition to be avoided, not a blessing to be embraced. Nationalization is a matter of practical choice rather than of hallowed doctrine. Keynesianism has superseded the old faith in a vast network of physical controls. The emphasis is on economic expansion, on the reform of education, on science and technology rather than on the old class-struggle war-cries. The Labour Party, which for a time threatened to break up into warring sects, has emerged from its troubles with unity restored and purpose fortified. Gaitskell's rôle in Britain in the 1950s was not unlike Adlai Stevenson's in the United States. Each led his party to the acceptance of new conditions and the perception of new truths; each adorned his leadership with a freshness of thought and a brilliance of exposition; each made it possible for his successor to move on from ancient feuds and exhausted controversies to confront the distinctive problems of the 1960s.

In liberating the Labour Party from the doctrines of the past, Gaitskell brought that party, I think, to a somewhat new view of the United States. In socialist demonology—even in social democratic demonology—America, as the presumed last citadel of *laissez-faire* capitalism, had a starring rôle. The testimony of London and Sinclair had been reinforced by Theodore Dreiser and Sinclair Lewis. For a time, Roosevelt and the New Deal muddled the clear images of Babbitry and reaction derived from the 'twenties; but, when the New Deal passed, the old stereotypes returned. The 1950s consolidated the picture of the United States as a bigoted and repressive nation, irrevocably conservative, given to the persecution of dissenters, the burning of books, and the protection of investments.

Gaitskell had his share of concern about tendencies in America in the early 'fifties. But he knew the United States to be a diverse land, filled with contradictions and possibilities; and he never for a moment accepted the thesis that it would for ever after be the bastion of reaction. He was confident that the progressive impulse was not dead, anticipated its revival and hoped that he could become its transatlantic partner. His belief in the potential strength of American democracy reinforced his conviction that the Atlantic Alliance was indispensable and the Atlantic Community indestructible.

As a consequence, Gaitskell was able to bring about close relations between the progressive politics of the two countries. This was a novel development. Though political moods in the two nations often ran along parallel lines, like parallel lines they never met. Even radical Americans, like the two Roosevelts, tended to have more intimate associations with progressive Tories than with Radicals or Socialists. The Liberal era in Britain and the Progressive era in the United States overlapped in the first two decades of the century. But, for all the intellectual and political affinities, personal contact was slight. Theodore Roosevelt detested the young Churchill. Woodrow Wilson distrusted Lloyd George. In the next reform era in the United States, the decade of the New Deal, contact was little closer. Franklin Roosevelt found Ramsay MacDonald at once fuzzy and doctrinaire; and he never could understand the post-MacDonald Labour Party which combined a rhetorical opposition to fascism with a practical opposition to rearmament. After the war, Harry Truman and Lord Attlee regarded each other with the mutual respect of one astute old pro for another, and Ernest Bevin won the affection of his opposite numbers in the field of foreign affairs; but even then the flow back and forth between the Labour Government and the Fair Deal was surprisingly meagre.

With Gaitskell this changed. He was bound by ties of intellectual interest and personal friendship with many liberal Democrats, and he had the liking of not a few liberal Republicans. His pragmatic conception of socialism enlisted sympathetic interest. He came often to Washington, was greeted with delight, and heard with respect. Though he had known President Kennedy only slightly as a Senator, he visited him on two occasions when he was President. Their conversation was intimate and wide-ranging, and they parted with mutual understanding and affection. When word of his death reached the United States, it was taken as a loss not only to England but to America. He was a good deal more than a national figure. Without becoming Prime Minister, he won international confidence as a man who nobly strove for the democratic purposes of decency, freedom, and justice in a world where those purposes seemed for a season under assault and in eclipse.

TWO PRIME MINISTERS SPEAK

1. Lord Attlee

I first heard of Hugh Gaitskell in the years succeeding the Labour defeat of 1931. I was at that time working with Stafford Cripps, Douglas Cole, and others in forming the Society for Socialist Information and Propaganda, and the Socialist League. There were a number of young university economists who were engaged in working out socialist policy. Hugh Gaitskell was one of them and I recall meeting him then. He was a good-looking man, obviously of great ability.

When I next came across him, he was working at the Board of Trade as a wartime temporary Civil Servant under Hugh Dalton who had the highest opinion of him. Elected MP for South Leeds in 1945, he was one of a group of new members such as Harold Wilson and Evan Durbin who were obviously destined for office, and he would have been appointed to an Under-secretaryship in the Labour Government but for a bout of ill-health. However, he had not long to wait before I sent him as Parliamentary Secretary to the Ministry of Fuel and Power. There he soon won the confidence of the miners, and a year later succeeded Mr. Shinwell as Minister.

Sir Stafford Cripps kept in close contact with a group of the younger Ministers. When in 1950 failing health was making him feel the strain of his office as Chancellor of the Exchequer and in effect Minister of Economic Planning, he asked if he could have the assistance of Gaitskell as Minister of State for Economic Affairs. Next year, when Sir Stafford had to retire, he strongly recommended Gaitskell as his successor. Although at forty-four he was young in years and, from the Parliamentary point of view, a very new member to hold what is considered to be the second place in the Government, I had no hesitation in accepting this advice. It required someone with real knowledge of finance to deal with the difficulties of the time. The effect of the Korean War was very adverse for Britain, a fact which was insufficiently appreciated by our American friends.

Gaitskell ran into difficulties over his first budget, where his proposal for checking the increasing cost of the Health Service brought him into conflict with Aneurin Bevan. Neither would give way, with the result that Bevan and Wilson left the Government. Gaitskell had here revealed his strength of character.

When the Labour Party went into Opposition, Gaitskell was naturally one of the leading figures on the Opposition Front Bench. He was regarded as being with Herbert Morrison on the right wing of the Party. When I decided that the time had come for my retirement, it was obvious that Gaitskell might be chosen as the outstanding figure among the younger men. I took no part in the choice of my successor, and it is wrong to suggest that I did anything to influence the party.

As leader of the party, Gaitskell had not a very easy time, but he showed great wisdom in coming to an agreement with Bevan, and up to the time of the latter's death they worked well together. I think that there was some danger in Gaitskell's tendency to associate closely with a group of personal friends and that he would have been wiser to have made wider contacts, but as by this time I was out of the House of Commons it may well be that I was mistaken. He was too, I think,

a little ill-advised to embark on an intended reform of the
basis of the party policy while he was at the same time having
to contend with the advocates of unilateral disarmament.

However, he overcame these difficulties and in the latter
years of his life grew in political stature. It was an error to
regard him as in any way a right-wing reactionary. Nor was
he a cold-blooded reactionary. In so much as these terms have
any validity, I should regard him as left of centre. Gaitskell
had wide international contacts and was very conscious of that
aspect of Labour policy. His untimely death revealed how
much he had impressed people by his firm character and
integrity. I have little doubt that had he survived he would
have made a very good prime minister. He was a tremendous
worker and never spared himself, indeed this devotion to duty
may have caused his premature death to the great loss of the
party, the country and the world.

2. *Walter Nash*

I first met Hugh Gaitskell in the flat of Hugh Dalton and his
wife at Ashley Gardens, Victoria, London, on the evening on
which King Edward VIII abdicated. It was 11 December, 1936,
and we listened together to the King's farewell broadcast.
Hugh Dalton had arranged for me to meet four of the younger
members of the Labour Party to discuss socialism and the
building of a better world. Those present were the late Evan
Durbin; Arthur Creech Jones (who was later to become
Secretary of State for the Colonies); John Wilmot (who later
became Lord Wilmot, and had just won Fulham at a famous
by-election); and Hugh Gaitskell.

We had a very happy, constructive, interesting evening, and I felt that Hugh Gaitskell and Evan Durbin (both of whom I met for the first time, having known Creech Jones and Wilmot before) had a great future in the Labour Movement, and that much benefit would come from the work of both of them. Unfortunately, Durbin lost his life much too soon, in a swimming accident.

On each subsequent occasion that I went to London and an opportunity was available, I met Hugh Gaitskell again, but mainly when he was Chancellor of the Exchequer and then after he was elected the leader of the party.

My most complete memory is of when I met him during the period of the Prime Ministers' Conference of 1962, and talked with him about the Common Market and the implications for Britain if she joined. These discussions were followed by discussions with representatives of the Commonwealth and socialists from the Common Market countries. They were completed by a conference of the Socialist International, with India added. I was privileged to be in London through the whole of these proceedings and it was the work of Hugh Gaitskell that brought them to unqualified conclusions and a final decision.

Hugh Gaitskell had great qualities and he won much respect. He was a little reserved. He never wasted words, but when he used them they were full of meaning and wisdom. Ranged with these qualities of a very high order, he had a kindly nature towards those with whom he had to deal. He had complete integrity. No one whom I have met more exemplified the advice of Polonius to Laertes: 'To thine own self be true, And it must follow, as the night the day, Thou canst not then be false to any man.'

He has gone, but mankind is better for his life. He was as great a man as I have known at any time.

THE INHERITANCE

David Wood

Within less than a year after Hugh Gaitskell's death the temptation must be strong in anybody who prized his friendship to recoil from cool assessment of his quality as a politician and party leader and to let the heart have its way in offering a warm memorial tribute to the man. The temptation is not less strong for a political correspondent who was close to him than for those who shared in his party commitments, his causes, and his fights and who became the more closely bound to him because his setbacks and victories were also theirs. Let me say, then, at the beginning that the remarkable quality in Hugh Gaitskell, as I knew him in private and studied him in public, was that he rang true under every test as few politicians find it possible to do and as some politicians do not particularly try to do. Everything he thought and did was out in the open, such was his integrity, and if ever one discovered his interests being protected or promoted by routine political intrigue, conspiracy, or caballing it could be traced back not to him but to the decision of his friends and well-wishers that they must do the dirty work for which he had so much intellectual contempt. Quite simply, it was impossible not to admire the standards of honesty and openness that he brought not merely to public life but to the rugged business of leading a political party—and a political party that at best is no more than a coalition of interests and at worst no more than rival factions.

No one need doubt that if his personal standards had been less strict, or just a little more expedient, his seven years as Labour leader would have been far easier. He could have made deals with his principal opponents within the party; most party leaders feel obliged to. He could have travelled by way of Birmingham to Beachy Head; most politicians do. He could have let others fight his causes inside the party and waited his time before he showed his own hand; Lord Attlee was a master of the technique. He did none of this. His battles had to be frontal battles. The party divisions on Clause Four and unilateral nuclear disarmament are the outstanding illustrations.

It needs no saying that in these frontal battles, in which at certain times he faced organized majority opinion within the party he led, Gaitskell showed a courage that gave him heroic proportions which even those who opposed him could not forbear to admire. Certainly in the country his stature grew as his support inside the Labour Party seemed to be fatally diminishing. Here, it was felt, stood a man who had virtues of guts and temperament of which authentic national leaders are made. Here was no time-server or trimmer of the kind who are twelve a penny in politics, but a man of spirit and resolute purpose. So the country began to see him. At that point Gaitskell began to make the subtle transition from politician to statesman.

But, for all one's admiration of the man, it was possible to wonder whether his virtues did not become a limitation. More than once in private sessions with Gaitskell I had to pose to myself the question whether his view of politics and party leadership was not more rigidly intellectual than was good either for his own comfort or perhaps for the unity of his party. To say that he was rigidly intellectual is certainly not to put another way Bevan's ludicrous charge that he was a desiccated calculating machine. Nobody who knew him, or had simply observed him in social settings, could fail to be aware that he was full of human warmth and compassion, with emotions quite near to the surface. Yet he never ceased to be an academic, a dealer in ideas. He did not like leaping instinctively to an answer, and when he did he could reach the politically inexpedient answer. He carried into politics his economist's need first to know the facts and then to move on from there along a purely rational plane. Once having reached his rational answer he did not easily change. He sometimes showed impatience if he thought himself obstructed by the unargued instincts or prejudices of those who relied less on rationalization, and now and then could go close to intellectual arrogance.

Two particular examples come to mind. Soon after the Anglo-French attack on Port Said, Gaitskell asked me how I had seen the troops on the spot reacting to the line he had taken in the House and the country. I was rather surprised that he should have thought that they, in their situation, should have much sympathy for it—simply because their country had committed them to what first promised to be a battle and they assumed the country would not undercut them for doing the job they had been ordered to do. He then said in a puzzled way that he had been taken aback by the many critical letters he had been sent at the time by ordinary working men in the factories (whose basic common sense and decency he always valued). To him the military operation deserved to be condemned on purely rational grounds; he made no allowance for the instinctive judgement that was certain to be made when British troops were sent into action, rightly or wrongly.

The other occasion concerns the Common Market and Gaitskell's attitude towards the Brussels negotiations. Through many months Gaitskell had given me the benefit of some brilliant and dispassionate assessments of the balance of advantage in going in or staying out, and he had left me with the clear impression that he thought the economic advantages were highly questionable but some political advantages fairly clear from the standpoint of Western unity and strength. We had another discussion after the Commonwealth Socialist leaders had met in London, but before both the Commonwealth Prime Ministers' conference and the Labour Party conference. I mentioned what I thought still to be his private position on the political advantages of British membership of the European Economic Community, and he very sharply corrected me. In the course of a sustained rationalization he firmly dismissed any suggestion that there would be political advantage in membership. But I later had reason to doubt whether in this instance the rationalization did not follow an emotional judgement, for he went on to say how deeply he had been moved by the fears of India and New Zealand as he had heard them expressed at the meeting of Commonwealth Socialist leaders. That meeting, I have no doubt, was decisive in Gaitskell's attitude towards the Brussels negotiations. A month later, at the party conference, he made what was widely reckoned to be the most cogent case so far put by a leading politician against going into EEC on any terms that the Government were likely to get. (He took this line in such a way that observers once again had to marvel at his scorn for political finesse: he savagely snubbed some of his most loyal followers who happened to be as European as they were Gaitskellite and gave the anti-Gaitskellite Left a sense that they had scored a victory.)

No, Hugh Gaitskell, as a lobby correspondent admiringly watched him, can hardly be presented as a master of the accepted techniques of party management. We have to admit that there was something in his temperament that caused him to try to get his way, not always out of necessity, by head-on collisions. Perhaps the worst misjudgement he made in party management was the provocation of controversy within the party over the revision of Clause 4 of the party constitution.

After all, he had been raised to the leadership essentially as the nominee of the trade union magnates, and the rock of his support in the Parliamentary Party for annual re-election as leader was to be found in the trade union groups of MPs. It was precisely in these quarters that Clause 4 was sentimentally valued, even if it were no longer taken literally. In the controversy that followed within the party, Gaitskell for once recognized that he had to retreat. He could not afford in the end to antagonize the supporters on whom he was simultaneously relying to fend off a party commitment to unilateralism. But if it has to be said that in crude terms of political expediency Gaitskell would have been wiser in his own and the party's interests not to let the controversy develop at that time and in that way, the fact that he did so paradoxically showed his quality as a man that in turn made his quality as a party leader whose influence, at the time of his death, spread far beyond his own party. For Gaitskell knew, as every one of his principal lieutenants and most of his rank and file knew, that Clause 4 was an anachronism and a dead letter. Hardly anybody thought it seriously meant what it said, although it remained on record both as a point of reference for opportunistic campaigns by the Labour Left and as an ammunition dump for political opponents. In all reason, then, why not get rid of it or amend it and say what the party really meant? Why not bring it into harmony with the spate (politically an excessive academic spate) of new policy documents that had flowed from Transport House between 1955 and 1959?

As this lobby correspondent followed the run of the play while Hugh Gaitskell fought to final victory his battle with Bevanism, in all its permutations, it was always important to remember with what glorious recklessness he could open his flanks to attack—by any of the ordinary political rules. This is why he allowed his two main most dangerous opponents their opportunity to challenge his position as leader, one inside the

Parliamentary Party and the National Executive Committee,
the other in the trade union world and at the party conference.
Take first Mr. Frank Cousins, the leader of the Transport and
General Workers' Union. By some accounts, Gaitskell just
before his death had begun to heal the breach with Cousins
and the two men might have eventually found a *modus vivendi*
that would have prevented further dangerously destructive
clashes. Yet it is no less puzzling than it ever was that Gaitskell,
for no obvious reason, did not at a very early stage go out of
his way to try to moderate the hostility of the most powerful
trade union leader in the movement. One got the impression
of two men, temperamentally at odds, who had set their faces
firmly against compromise, although neither had the right
kind of power completely to break the other, so that all they
could hurt was their common cause. Then take Mr. Wilson,
who has succeeded to the leadership. Search as hard as one
likes it is hard to find firm evidence that Gaitskell and Wilson
differed on the essentials of opposition to a unilateralist commitment; they differed rather on the method by which the
unilateralist challenge on party policy should be tackled. This
difference developed until Mr. Wilson felt justified in standing
in the leadership election to test the strength of opposition to
Gaitskell inside the Parliamentary Party, into whose keeping
the leader had committed his future with thoroughly justified
confidence, at the 1960 conference, in his 'fight and fight and
fight again' speech. On a purely political level, then, it had
occasionally to be asked at the time whether Gaitskell might
not have done more to prevent both Cousins and Wilson from
being drawn so far into the anti-Gaitskellite camp.

Yet this observer, for one, could never feel that the political
level, where conflicting interests and ambitions are reconciled
in a bargain and where issues are burked by compromise,
mattered most. It seemed supremely important, throughout
the years of Gaitskell's leadership, that the Labour Party, as the

alternative government, should prepare itself, or by force of one man's character become prepared, for the day when it would return to office by clearing its mind of fog and confusion on some of the fundamentals of foreign policy. There were plenty of siren voices in the Labour Party warning Gaitskell that what mattered above all was unity; but Gaitskell saw that it mattered most what the party was united on, and he was prepared to pass through a tremendous personal ordeal and to subject his party to very dangerous strains to make sure that in the end it united on what he passionately believed to be right policies. This was true leadership of a kind we rarely see. It was a cruel irony that he should have died just as his struggles, at least temporarily, were ending and when his personal authority in his party and his stature in the country were at their zenith.

The effects of the protracted and bitter internal struggle on Gaitskell were of more than one kind. I always doubted whether he ever had any strong temperamental liking for political cut and thrust, or any natural aggressiveness, for he was not only a highly rational man but a sensitive man who could be easily pierced by barbed words. But his days had to be spent in two running battles—with his political opponents and with many of those who were theoretically his supporters. Nobody had cause to be surprised if in this awful environment he tended to become more and more remote, as he seemed to me to do, except with those on whose loyalty he knew he could unreservedly count. This exposed him to the charge of leading a clique within the party. I had no doubt, either, that circumstances obliged him to overwork cruelly; he could not confidently delegate work so much as would have been advisable, both in the interests of his own health and of the self-esteem of his principal lieutenants.

That was predictably one side of the medal. There was another side. The ordeal which he steeled himself to endure

heightened his powers and toughened his fibre. His parliamentary speeches as a Minister up to 1951 were always notable for
lucidity of thought and clarity of exposition; and his Budget
speech as Chancellor of the Exchequer, when he was forty-
four, gave no reason for anyone to think that there had been a
fall from the exceptional standard set by Sir Stafford Cripps.
But his speeches since the 1959 General Election had taken on a
different quality. He was no more a phrasemaker or a wit than
he had ever been; he relied as before, on the force of reason
and narrative power. But there was a marked growth in the
authority of his style and increasingly frequent undertones of
passion. He had reached the point where on foreign affairs he
spoke for more than his party; he had become one of the key
voices of England. If this development was noticeable in the
House, so it was noticeable outside. There are not a few
political reporters who say that some of the finest speeches they
have heard in recent years were those delivered by Gaitskell,
in the teeth of the gale of opposition at recent party conferences.

The same growth in authority and stature made its impress
in private. Those who saw him regularly could not fail to be
aware towards the end that they were in the presence of an
evolving statesman who had potentialities of greatness. His
contempt for the cruder parts of the political game seemed to
increase; and I remember not only the candour with which he
would use the phrase 'fellow travellers' of a few party members, but also the pleasure with which he would show how he
had been impressed by the common-sense abilities of some
party member with whom he had not before sensed any
affinity. As always he could be relied upon to give the most
balanced and dispassionate assessment of economic trends to be
found in Westminster politics. He seemed to enjoy being
judicial and academic, rather than partisan, on this his special
subject, and there were some occasions when it seemed to

me that the Treasury would have benefited from knowing his private reading of the short-term and mid-term future. His predictions maintained a remarkable accuracy, as well as scrupulous fairness of mind about the policies of his opponents.

To look back on Gaitskell's political years is to be baffled by the paradox that a man with so much talent and appetite for friendship and fellow feeling, with so much sensitiveness and tolerant compassion, should have had to spend what might have been his most creative political years in bitter feuds with members of his own party. Remembering many conversations we had on the basis of Lobby protocol from which I do not consider his death sets me free, I have no reasonable doubt where the explanation lay. Gaitskell, though not shorter on modesty than most politicians, strongly believed that he was better fitted to judge the interests of his country and his party than many of his followers who responded like Pavlov's dogs to the ring of certain predictable bells; and the time came when he knew that as an Englishman and a democratic socialist he had to save the Labour movement from the fatal consequences of its own sentiment. By his elevation to the leadership he became the standard-bearer, as he saw himself, of the decent, right-minded traditional strain in British socialism, which is gradualist and not revolutionary, tolerant and not extreme, idealistic but not woolly. As the standard-bearer he became the principal target of extreme and impatient socialists. What remains remarkable, when we remember how he bore the full force of the virulence of those to whom he was at times the only ultimate obstacle, is that his integrity was never touched. Let a political correspondent testify that from beginning to end of the internal disputes in which he became involved he did justice to his opponents. In privately explaining some aspect of the controversy he would give an account of his opponent's views no less full and punctilious than he gave his own. (I remember how characteristically he summed up Dick

Crossman's value to the Labour Party when Crossman left the front bench for the back benches; nor did I ever hear him say an ungenerous thing about Harold Wilson when he made a challenge for the leadership.) Gaitskell could not help believing that in the end every judgement must run with the force of reasonable argument, and therefore he could not believe that he damaged his own interests by being fair to those who argued against him. Within my experience, at least, this carried a reward. The party controversies had their savage phases, when the Queensberry rules were abandoned, but in my hearing nobody ever assailed Gaitskell's character or questioned the honesty of his motives in anything he said or did. It was impossible not to conclude that by sheer force of his character he compelled every stage of the battle to be fought where he wanted it fought, on the plane of reason; and the most implacable adversary he had could do no worse than say that Gaitskell's reasoning did not satisfy him.

For a political journalist friendship with Gaitskell offered a rare experience. It seems when a journalist enters the trade that it will be a world in which there is a constant play of ideas. But he soon learns that the intellectual content of politics today, whatever it once was, is thin, as anybody may see from the next pamphlet or policy statement put out by any of the political parties. Hugh Gaitskell was a genuine dealer in ideas, a contributor to the intellectual content of politics of his time as well as its practice, as Harold Macmillan and R. A. Butler can be and as, in his aberrant way, Dick Crossman is. And I for one do not believe that Gaitskell's very English intellectual interpretation of what democratic socialism is, or should be, has died with him. The works and the influence of an expedient politician may end when he ends; the force of reason is no less valid when the voice has gone.

LIST OF ILLUSTRATIONS

The cartoon by Vicky on page 132 appeared in the *News Chronicle* on 20 October, 1950

INDEX